The *Bohemian Modern* home is a place where creativity, individuality, and a wild mix of colour and pattern meet in a modern environment. Emily Henson starts by taking a look at the different facets of the look: pattern and colour, textiles, handmade pieces, living with plants, and collections and display. She also offers styling tricks to use at home and ideas for recycling and reuse. Next, a series of case studies take a closer look at free-spirited and creative homes and the people who live in them. From a restored barn on the coast of Morocco to a former parking garage in the Netherlands that's been converted into a flexible live/work space, Emily shows that any home can have *Bohemian Modern* style.

Bohemian
MODERN

Bohemian
MODERN

Emily Henson

Photography by
Katya de Grunwald

RYLAND PETERS & SMALL
LONDON • NEW YORK

SENIOR DESIGNER Toni Kay
SENIOR COMMISSIONING EDITOR
Annabel Morgan
LOCATION RESEARCH Jess Walton
PRODUCTION Gordana Simakovic
ART DIRECTOR Leslie Harrington
EDITORIAL DIRECTOR Julia Charles
PUBLISHER Cindy Richards

First published in 2015.
This revised edition published in 2020
by Ryland Peters & Small
20–21 Jockey's Fields,
London WC1R 4BW
and
341 E 116th Street
New York, NY 10029
www.rylandpeters.com

Text copyright © Emily Henson
2015, 2020
Design and photographs copyright
© Ryland Peters & Small 2015, 2020

10 9 8 7 6 5 4 3 2 1

ISBN 978-1-78879-286-8

A CIP record for this book
is available from the British Library.

Library of Congress CIP data
has been applied for.

Printed and bound in China

CONTENTS

INTRODUCTION

BELOW LEFT In this Danish family home, a garden designer has mixed 'granny chic' florals with Moroccan rugs and framed posters for a quirky and stylish bohemian look.

BELOW RIGHT An architect and artist built this Dutch home from the ground up. They have flawlessly blended old and new, sleek and rough, for a rustic bohemian style.

I first had the idea for *Bohemian Modern* when I was travelling in Los Angeles for my first book. It was sparked in part by a resurgence in that ancient knotting technique that was popular in the 1970s – macramé. I kid you not, everywhere I looked people were doing it. This craft that my mother's generation was probably so glad to see the back of was making my own generation go bananas. Oversized macramé wall hangings, mini macramé necklaces, plant holders, bed canopies and dog coats (OK, I made that last one up, but I'm certain they exist). I tried my hand at it, and I admit it was fun. Kind of like my favourite childhood game, Cat's Cradle, but with a prize at the end: a plant holder! The 1970s were having a comeback, and as a child of the '80s I was into it.

I became curious about people who were taking those ideas made popular in the 1970s and rethinking them for today's world. Not just macramé but also houseplants en masse, boucherouite rugs and, dare I say it, dream catchers – basically, all those clichéd ideas that spring to mind when you think of 1970s interiors. I had lived in Los Angeles for many years and had seen the style

re-emerge in the hills of Echo Park, home to many new bohemians seeking a liberated and creative lifestyle. I set out to find modern homes that fitted this idea of 21st-century bohemian, but what I found instead was a group of individuals who tick the Bohemian Modern box not just because their homes scream 'modern hippy' (although some do) but because they are actually living a Bohemian Modern lifestyle – creative, unconventional and shunning the status quo in interiors, and doing so with such flair and success. They are bohemian in spirit, not just in style.

For *Bohemian Modern*, I travelled Europe to share with you the homes of artists, architects and designers of all kinds, from furniture and interiors to textiles and gardens. I certainly saw my fair share of macramé and kilim rugs, as you might expect in a bohemian home, but more excitingly I also saw innovation and creativity in the homeowners' interiors choices. They proved to be free spirits who refuse to follow the rules, choosing instead to make up their own. I finished my travels feeling truly inspired and reinvigorated in my own work as a stylist and designer.

BELOW LEFT In a Moroccan riad, white-washed walls provide a clean canvas for the homeowner's collection of retro furniture – not what you expect to find within the walls of the ancient medina.

BELOW RIGHT Polished limestone plaster coats the floors in this lakeside home near Amsterdam. Corners are filled with plants, and the neutral base is broken up by the orange plastic chairs, found in the junk.

THE
DETAILS

Pattern and colour

I've always been drawn to vibrant colours and patterns. Although I've toned it down in recent years, I still tend to choose colour over neutral and print over plain. When I think of a bohemian home, this is what springs to mind. Not that every Bohemian Modern home has a vibrant colour palette – you will see in the case studies that some don't – but very often it is a defining element. Whether they are introduced via textiles, paint, tiles or wallpaper, pattern and colour are great starting points for a room's décor, and a foundation upon which to build a strong look.

RIGHT In this stylish open-plan living space, a feminine floral rug is the perfect contrast to the pop of yellow on the freestanding 'wall'. Hidden within the yellow panelling are the utility pipes from the kitchen below. What could have been unsightly has been cleverly disguised and built into a stunning feature.

OPPOSITE ABOVE LEFT A woven plastic stair runner in red and white zigzags provides a playful contrast to the worn brick walls of this stairway.

OPPOSITE ABOVE RIGHT A plastic rug is paired with a mini plastic pouffe. These rugs are a colourful and practical addition to the Bohemian Modern home – great both indoors and out, and easily cleaned.

OPPOSITE BELOW LEFT A glossy red kitchen shelf holds a selection of eye-catching cans and packages. Frequently used items such as coffee and tea can easily be decanted into more attractive containers.

OPPOSITE BELOW RIGHT A vibrant mix of patterned pillows – some handmade, some store-bought – livens up a plain bed.

ABOVE LEFT A removable baby gate prevents tumbles from this custom-built bunk bed. Its interior is painted a shocking acid yellow, a fun contrast to the geometric pink blanket.

ABOVE RIGHT In this children's room, a lacquered apple green dresser doubles as a handy changing table. It provides a lively jolt of colour against the watery blue wall.

BELOW RIGHT Chunky corduroy may not be the first thing you think of in a Bohemian Modern home, but when a boxy chair is covered in a hot pink shade, it is current and stylish, particularly when partnered with a blue-grey wall and a folksy cushion.

OPPOSITE From the interior courtyard of this Moroccan riad, a door leads to a bedroom. Although many different patterned tiles have been used, the restricted palette of greys, blues and greens keeps the overall feel calm and tranquil.

THIS MAY NOT BE GROUND-BREAKING INFORMATION, but it's worth remembering that choosing a colour story and trying to stick to it can make or break a room. A stripe, an Ikat print and a chevron can live side by side if they are all in complementary shades of blue, grey and green, for example, but if each individual pattern is also in a different colour, it can feel too chaotic. You can mix together as many patterns as you want, as long as they share a similar group of colours.

But here's where I contradict myself, because the flip side of this so-called rule is that 'every colour in the rainbow' is also a

THIS PAGE If these tiles were white, imagine how different this kitchen would feel. When your kitchen cabinets are shades of white or grey, you can transform the room with a single-coloured tile backdrop. Sometimes all you need is one strong colour in a room, and it pays to be bold.

ABOVE LEFT In this Moroccan kitchen, things are kept organic with exclusively handmade ceramic wares on display. Glazed in shades of green, blue and yellow, they tie in beautifully with the rest of the home's décor.

ABOVE RIGHT Alternating between solid and patterned tiles, this staircase in a Moroccan riad is covered top to bottom in colour. However, a palette of blues and greens has been strictly adhered to throughout the interior, for a cohesive and calming effect.

perfectly acceptable colour story in the Bohemian Modern home. Sometimes it works to go over the top, but be prepared for a lively home. If you can get the balance right, multi-coloured craziness can work. You wouldn't guess it now from looking at my fairly subdued living room (see pages 108–115), but there was a time, a few years ago, when I had a multitude of different hues in my house – furniture, textiles and art were all wildly colourful. What kept it from feeling too overpowering (although it came very close to the line) were the white walls and floorboards. This calm, whitewashed backdrop allowed me to go a bit crazy with everything else while avoiding the carnival look.

Because I'm drawn to colour and pattern mostly through textiles, I prefer to keep my walls white or a very soft off-white shade. It means that I can alter the whole look of a room just by changing the cushions or curtains or bedding. But you may prefer to bathe yourself in every imaginable shade of blue, green, pink and yellow, in which case forgo the neutral base altogether and paint your walls in clashing colours. When viewed side by side, rooms painted in different colours are great fun, and when patterns are layered on top it can be a winning look, as long as you exercise a little restraint. Paint can have a huge impact on a space and it's relatively inexpensive and easy to do it yourself. If coating your walls in vivid colours feels like a step too far, try painting one piece of furniture in a dramatic shade, and preferably in a high-gloss or lacquer finish, to keep it modern.

Textiles

For as long as I can remember I've had a thing for textiles. From an early age, I would scour jumble sales and charity shops/thrift stores, picking up scraps of fabric or sometimes dresses and scarves, always with the intention of turning them into something for my room and later my home. A basket of fabric holds endless possibilities for me – just a few yards of material can be swiftly transformed into a bedspread, curtains, cushions or a slipcover. Textiles are at the heart of the Bohemian Modern home, whether plain and textured or patterned and fringed.

RIGHT In this Danish home, an antique bench is tucked under the stairs, creating a seating nook with a view to the garden. A Juju hat – a feathered ceremonial headdress from Cameroon – adorns the wall above a set of cushions made from antique kilim rugs. An angular standard lamp by Italian lighting brand Artemide adds a contemporary touch.

OPPOSITE ABOVE LEFT In this bright sunroom, piles of sheepskins and long-haired goatskins make for a cosy reading nook.

OPPOSITE ABOVE RIGHT These homeowners have gone for the more-is-more approach, combining colour and pattern in their giant floor cushions. Vintage blankets can easily be sewn into floor cushion covers.

OPPOSITE BELOW LEFT In this outside 'room', the owner's old bed has been converted into a sofa and layered with cushions made from pieces of kilim rug patchworked together.

OPPOSITE BELOW RIGHT This stool came with the appliquéd chevron design already in place, but it would be easy enough to replicate to add pattern to a plain blanket or cushion.

ABOVE RIGHT Rugs and other textiles can have major impact when hung on the wall. In this Belgian townhouse, an antique piece has been hung next to the fireplace on a simple wooden dowel. Another way of hanging a rug without damaging is by Velcro tape, the loop side of the tape carefully sewn by hand to the back of the textile and the adhesive hook side attached to the wall.

MY LOVE OF TEXTILES STARTED when I was about seven years old and my mum opened an antique clothing shop in West London called Nostalgia. For the next few years, I spent every day after school in the large changing room, trying on 1930s bed jackets in peachy satin, and colourful tulle petticoats from the 1950s, daydreaming in front of the mirror with the lightbulbs around the frame. I loved the feeling of the fabric in my hand, so much more luxurious than the polyester of my 1970s childhood. It's a wonder I didn't go into fashion. When I was a little older, I became more interested in interiors, and instead of wearing the vintage scarves my mum would buy for her shop, I would 'borrow' them and pin them onto my bedroom wall like a piece of art.

There are so many ways to bring textiles into the Bohemian Modern home, from the obvious choices of rugs and cushions to less-expected ones such as wall hangings and children's teepees. Re-imagining uses for textiles is important too: rugs don't only belong on the floor; a sheepskin or kilim will make an effective cover-up for a worn armchair or can add colour and comfort to a plain sofa. By layering cushions in varying patterns and

THIS PAGE The walls of this bedroom are kept white to offset the many patterned textiles. The textiles and the art are all in natural, earthy shades, including the headboard, which the owner covered herself by sewing a very basic slipcover from a favourite vintage fabric. The wooden lamp is by Muuto.

A child's bedroom in Morocco could have felt cold and sterile with its *tadelakt* (lime plaster) floors and shelves, but warmed up with a multi-coloured boucherouite rug and a star-smattered tepee, it's playful and cosy. Boucherouite rugs are usually made in the rag rug style from various textiles and are easily cleaned, so perfect for kids' rooms.

textures, you can create an inviting and eclectic place to hunker down with a book. A striking rug can also become a focal point when displayed on a wall. Hung above a sofa or on a blank wall, it's an easy way to elevate a room – minimum effort, maximum impact.

Whether you sew or not, fabric bought by the metre/yard has so much potential. I learned how to sew when I was pregnant with my now 15-year-old daughter, and I still use the same machine. It's worth learning even the most basic stitch, as it opens up a world of possibilities in DIY interiors. If you can't or don't want to learn, it's easy enough to find

someone to do the work for you. There are also plenty of no-sew ways to use textiles, such as stapling or even just tucking fabric over a tired seat or draping a tapestry over a chair back. You can also stretch some onto a canvas or frame it, creating instant wall art. Every home should have a stash of textiles on hand for when a quick update is needed.

LEFT In this Danish home, a vintage kilim rug adds texture to an otherwise sleek corner. A 1960s chair has been upholstered in men's pinstripe suiting fabric, while the homeowner's own photography is displayed on glass panels behind.

ABOVE In my living room, I dyed a piece of grey linen using the Japanese *shibori* technique. I sewed a channel at the top and hung it on a wooden dowel. I also dyed some extra fabric to make cushions.

Contrast

I've always been a bit obsessed with the idea of contrast in interiors. Different materials, colours, patterns and eras are what make a home interesting. In a Bohemian Modern home it is more important than ever, and the key to making the boho modern is contrast. Layered kilims and suzani textiles are what you might expect for a traditional bohemian look, but adding a jolt of bold neon or the gleam of slick copper takes an interior into the realm of the unexpected. And for me, a home looks its most compelling when things are unpredictable, imperfect and slightly off-kilter.

RIGHT In this 18th-century townhouse, a large room has been converted into a very stylish B&B. An empty alcove has been clad in beautifully grained plywood to create an unexpected feature. Styles collide, with a Saarinen chair beside a cane armchair and a makeshift rough-hewn plant stand. The offbeat look is completed with a child's painted heart.

OPPOSITE ABOVE LEFT In this Dutch home, a group of disparate items somehow makes sense. Although of different eras and styles, they create their own unique look.

OPPOSITE ABOVE RIGHT In my own bedroom, metallics enliven the built-in cupboards. Slick copper lighting and pewter candleholders provide contrast to the room's Victorian details.

OPPOSITE BELOW LEFT An original 18th-century fresco dominates this grand staircase, but instead of using antique furniture, a neon block of wood and a crackled metal chair add a touch of modern cool.

OPPOSITE BELOW RIGHT A vibrant curtain and jungly plants enliven this sterile bathroom, testament to the fact that a few quick fixes can make all the difference.

ABOVE Despite its bright hue, the yellow clock case provides a quiet moment within a fun jumble of pattern and colour. The chairs were upholstered in a collection of colourful old jumpers by the homeowner's mother.

ZIGZAGGING ACROSS EUROPE for the photography of this book, one of the things I noticed was how well many of the homeowners mixed contrasting ideas in their homes. There seemed to be a universal dismissal of the 'rules' that typically dictate the way in which we decorate our interiors. Just because one homeowner lives with his family in an 18th-century Belgian townhouse complete with original frescoes doesn't mean that he has to decorate in the Rococo style – and he certainly does not. And the fact that another lives in a 19th-century factory doesn't dictate that she must shop only at antiques markets. I've never understood the idea of sticking to one style if you like many, or buying, for example, a mid-century modern home and decorating it only in furniture from that era. For me it becomes too much of a time warp, a museum, and I don't like the limitations it enforces. I say break the rules and start mixing it up!

To create interest in a home, there needs to be the right balance of varying elements: hard versus soft; warm versus cold; old versus new; masculine versus feminine; pattern versus plain, and so on. If you have inherited a bathroom that is all stainless steel and white tiles, this is the perfect opportunity to add softness and warmth with a patterned curtain beneath the sink and a cluster of lush plants to breathe life into a stark room. Or perhaps you would like some vintage furniture in your boho home but you don't want things to feel too retro. In which case, suspending a disco ball from the ceiling or painting one major piece of furniture in a bold gloss hue can lift a room out of the past and straight into the present day. Finding the right balance of contrast in your home can be tricky, but it's worth the trouble for the end result: a quirky, striking and brave bohemian style.

JAZZFES
BERLIN?
Haus der Berliner Festspiele,
Quasimodo, A-Trane,
Georg-Neumann-Saal, Savoy Berlin
3. BIS 7. NOVEMBER Unter Beteiligung der Hörfunker
Künstlerischer Leiter Nils Lan
TEL. 030-25489100 WWW.JAZZFEST-B
Berliner Festspiele

THIS PAGE Floor-to-ceiling industrial shelving provides
ample space for this Belgian family's many books
and keepsakes; it also divides the long living room,
creating separate seating areas within the open-plan
space. The sofa is upholstered in fabric by Vlisco.

Bring the outdoors in

There is something about plants that brings a room to life. They are wondrous things that can make the difference between a space that is ordinary and one that wows. If you were to look at photos of a room before and after plants were added, you would swear that more had changed. They have a truly transformative power when it comes to interiors. Houseplants have definitely made a comeback in recent years, and they are a vital part of the Bohemian Modern home. I know, I know, I can hear it now: 'I don't have green fingers'… 'I forget to water them'. But fear not, there are ways around this.

OPPOSITE ABOVE LEFT **A** collection of mounted wooden frames is a simple way to display tiny potted plants and favourite miniatures. Presented in this way, the plants themselves become the art.

OPPOSITE ABOVE RIGHT Concrete planters are cradled by macramé pot holders, handmade by the homeowner from neon string.

OPPOSITE BELOW LEFT This shelf was made from a piece of painted wood and leather shoelaces, and holds an ever-changing selection of cuttings, shells and plants.

OPPOSITE BELOW RIGHT Sometimes all you need is a couple of huge sculptural plants to liven up a room. This one seems to be very happy in its sun-drenched corner.

RIGHT Because of the open-plan nature of this huge home, special attention has been taken to creating 'rooms' where in fact there are none. Here, a group of plants, anchored by a huge yellow wire floor lamp, creates a soft barrier between areas.

RIGHT Keep an eye out for branches in interesting shapes and then do what I do – embarrass your kids by dragging them home from the park. Here, a tall beauty is propped in the corner and used to hang small plants.

FAR RIGHT In this Moroccan home, an alcove above an old well is adorned with a cluster of holey stones hung on a string. Look out for stones with holes in them – a fun project for a day at the seaside, with or without kids.

OPPOSITE It's no surprise to learn that a garden designer lives in this airy Danish home. The cane chairs and floral armchair already give the room a sense of the outdoors, but with the addition of so much plant life, it begins to feel like an exotic greenhouse.

FOR AS LONG AS I HAVE HAD MY OWN HOME, I have filled it with greenery. Even in my university dorm room, I had a huge potted plant that I somehow managed not to kill in between studying and partying. When my husband and I moved into our first apartment together, it was a tiny place above a garage in a Spanish-style building in Burbank, California. The apartment was small but it had a huge covered patio that was more like another room. I was heavily pregnant, working at a job I didn't like and feeling a bit down in the dumps when I woke one morning to find the whole space filled with plants and flowers. My husband had got up at dawn and

gone to LA's flower district to surprise me and cheer me up. Since then I have always had plants at home, and my children have grown up knowing that when I'm away they have to keep them alive! I'm not going to lie, there have been a few casualties.

There are so many easy-to-maintain options, from the waxy leafed fig tree to cacti to a rosemary cutting from your neighbour's garden (shh, don't tell!) that anyone can enjoy a bit of indoor gardening. In the Bohemian Modern home, there are no rules when it comes to plants. A spiky aloe vera can sit next to trailing ivy and glossy ficus. I tend to go for the more-is-more approach, lining

OPPOSITE With its modern practicality, the Bucketlight, by Dutch designer Roderick Vos, is the perfect foil for the antique armoire and mounted plate collection on the rough brick wall behind. This combined plant pot and light fixture, made from powder-coated cast aluminium, is an unusual way to introduce both plants and ambience into a home.

ABOVE RIGHT This plant is literally reaching for the sky as it grows up the wall towards a skylight. Apparently, it was on its last legs, but a change of scene has allowed it to thrive.

RIGHT This stunning plant is an imposter. It is a brilliant fake, handmade from painted paper and purchased at a student art fair. The homeowners are designers and professors who obviously have a good sense of humour. It certainly fooled me.

windowsills, mantelpieces and the tops of cabinets with pots. But one big sculptural potted tree works just as well. Succulents and cacti are good options if you won't remember to water them as often as you should. I had them in always-hot LA and I have them in usually-cold London, and they have survived in both places. And if you really feel that you are an incurable plant killer, there are some very convincing fakes available nowadays – not the cheesy silk flowers or unnaturally green 'ferns' that probably come to mind.

Almost as important as the plants are the containers in which they sit. You can't go wrong with simple terracotta, which suits a boho home really well, but for a more modern look, go for concrete planters or colourful woven baskets in geometric patterns. Or try your hand at a macramé hanging basket, giving it an update by using neon or black string instead of twine. In all honesty, anything can become a vessel for plants. One of the homeowners I've featured uses everything from seaside buckets to plastic drinks bottles to large vegetable oil drums in which to plant his cuttings. Once you start looking, you will find original plant pot ideas everywhere. Whatever you choose, whether real or artificial plants, macramé or concrete pots, I promise you that plants will be the icing on your home, that final layer that makes it feel complete and alive (and delicious).

Collections

Collections aren't usually planned. Often what happens is you find something that catches your eye, maybe a heart-shaped stone, a vintage vase or a Chinese lantern, and then a few weeks later you find another. Once you stumble upon your third, it's hard to resist the feeling of serendipity and, if you are anything like me, a collection is born. A Bohemian Modern home wouldn't be complete without a collection or two. They are an authentic expression of what the homeowner holds dear, and a window on their view of the world, in a way that furniture and other belongings aren't.

OPPOSITE ABOVE LEFT **A** shelf tucked under the stairs is home to a growing collection of bits found in nature, most of them gathered close to this Moroccan beachside home.

OPPOSITE ABOVE RIGHT **Hidden** amidst the climbing vines in this warehouse is a collection of terracotta and metal objects, and some made by the product designer who lives here.

OPPOSITE BELOW LEFT **A** collection of vases and blankets stands on top of a dresser, the items linked by their common colours and patterns.

OPPOSITE BELOW RIGHT **In** the pantry of this home, a collection of mismatched and mostly handmade bowls is grouped together. Not all collections are for display only; some are meant to be used day to day.

RIGHT These homeowners have found the perfect high–low balance in their home, mixing plush vintage rugs with rough-hewn African stools and classic designer chairs. The same can be said of their collection, which blends Holmegaard vases with pieces of coral and paint samples from their latest interiors projects, all beautiful in their own way.

RIGHT This is the home of self-confessed, die-hard collectors. They now have the space to spread out in this vast home and finally display all their collections. In their very large kitchen, an entire brick wall is given over to a huge array of antique blue-and-white china.

OPPOSITE In this cheerful dining room, two collections live side by side. The first portrait on the peachy wall was found on a trip to Indonesia; the others were later sourced by family and via the internet. The cluster of pretty pastel-hued Chinese lanterns was picked up on a trip to New York's Chinatown.

I'VE ALWAYS BEEN A COLLECTOR, some might say of completely useless junk. But I am a great believer in that old saying 'One man's junk…' I will admit, however, that in the past I've collected things that come pretty close to being considered junk (jam jars, anyone?).

I often wonder if I became a stylist because I'm a collector, or if I'm a collector because I'm a stylist. It's a job that requires a fair amount of stuff (I euphemistically like to call my stuff 'props', because it makes me feel better), and I've always had that magpie trait

OPPOSITE Animal skulls of every size hang from floor to ceiling in this Moroccan home. Some were found on the beach and in fields nearby, others in antique shops and gifted by generous friends.

BELOW LEFT Trinkets and pompoms – bits we accumulate and don't quite know what to do with – hang prettily on a doorknob.

BELOW CENTRE A jumble of painted loom weights makes a fitting collection for a purveyor of antique Morcoccan rugs.

BELOW RIGHT In a vast wall of windows, many collections are displayed, including these wooden walking sticks.

of being attracted to shiny objects. But the great thing about collections is that they aren't about usefulness; they are about beauty, and your very own version of beauty, no less.

A collection means different things to different people: some people collect art, some collect plates, others collect rocks. There's no right or wrong. At the end of the day, if it's a group of related items that you love displayed together, it's a collection. I saw some lovely examples as I travelled for this book – colourful woven plastic flasks in Amsterdam, feathers, fossils and animal skulls in Morocco and vintage glassware in Belgium. There are so many ways to source things today, from eBay to Etsy, that if you find yourself wanting to grow a collection, the internet now connects the entire world. I'm more old school, preferring a good rummage

at a market in the hopes of finding something perfect and unexpected to add to my hoard.

I heard from some of the homeowners in this book how friends and family all over the globe help with their collections. Friends do like to get involved, but be warned: if you announce that you love elephants, you might soon be inundated with all manner of elephants, big and small, and perhaps some you might not have chosen yourself...

It's important to be thoughtful when it comes to displaying collections. A large group of animal skulls looks stunning hung en masse on a wall; a few on a mantelpiece simply wouldn't have the same effect. Containment is important with collections, so utilize cabinets and shelves, devoting them entirely to a collection to make a statement. More is usually more, but make it artful and purposeful.

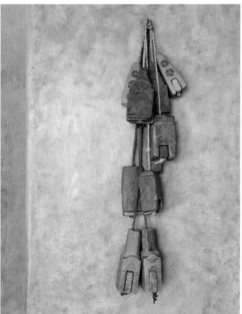

Styling

I've always been a stylist, even before I was actually doing it professionally. Any opportunity to rearrange furniture or help decorate in some way, and I was there. Now that I have been styling for a living for many years, I've learned a few tricks that are just as useful at home as they are on set. But let's not pretend that we all live in a photographic studio, where everything is perfect and hours are spent to get the shot just right. Your home is not a showroom and styling it should be fun, simply another way to display your favourite things artfully.

RIGHT This room already has two sofas, so it didn't need another. Instead, the designer who lives here created a smartly styled moment with vintage folding chairs, a chest and a huge painting (her own work). It probably doesn't get used often, but it is a beautiful overflow seating area when needed. The rug helps define the area.

OPPOSITE ABOVE LEFT On top of a glossy black piano, treasured items are styled together, making a statement against the peachy pink wall. The black bass guitar is part of the styled collection, and the pink walls are echoed in the framed print.

OPPOSITE ABOVE RIGHT An empty corner comes to life thanks to a few black-and-white photos and some kilim cushions.

OPPOSITE BELOW LEFT A mood board is another way to help you style your bits and pieces. As well as helping formulate your ideas, they can become works of art in their own right.

OPPOSITE BELOW RIGHT Sitting up high in the kitchen is this alcove, out of reach from little curious hands and the perfect spot for a styled moment of precious ornaments and art.

I BRIEFLY CONSIDERED CALLING THIS CHAPTER ANTI-STYLING, but I thought that might be confusing. What I mean is that I rebel against perfection. In my commercial work as a stylist, I work very hard to make it look as if a set hasn't been styled at all, almost as if someone has just got up and walked out of the room, leaving a bit of a mess in her wake. A shot of a desk is so much more refreshing if there is a pile of crumpled paper on the floor; and a living room is only more inviting if the sofa cushions are messed up and there's a rumpled throw spilling onto the floor. So when I talk about styling here, I'm not suggesting that we should all live in immaculate, spotless homes where nothing is out of place. That's not realistic and it's also very boring. The most interesting and welcoming homes are those with what I like to call 'signs of life', not those where you are afraid to sit on the sofa for fear of spoiling the cushion arrangement.

ABOVE This homeowner has a great eye for colour, sticking to neutral earthy tones and mixing them with metallics for a pleasing effect. The round wooden shelf is an excellent choice for its style and practicality – all those tiny treasures we amass are given a home – and ties in with the wooden Muuto lamp.

Styling your favourite bits and pieces can be a nice way to add life to forgotten areas. Pay attention to wasted spaces in your home and re-imagine their uses. Most of us have a cabinet or shelf, a windowsill or ledge that's crying out for a little collection of small treasures, curated and styled by you. There are so many opportunities for creating styled vignettes in a home, although I personally tend to forgo the obvious ones like coffee tables or any other spot that gets a lot of use.

For me it's a losing battle to attempt to have pretty things on the coffee table when, let's be honest, what really ends up there are piles of magazines, television remotes, toys and other random bits and pieces. If anything, a beautiful tray and some nice lidded boxes to catch the life junk are all I have, at least during this child-rearing phase of my life.

But consider areas like the top of an upright piano, or a kitchen shelf too high to be easily accessible yet perfect for a group of plants,

THIS PAGE I make no excuses for the clutter around my dressing table. I style up things I use daily – make-up, perfume, jewellery – with things I like to look at – art, photos, plants. I found this dresser on the street and made my kids help carry it home, much to their horror.

RIGHT On this landing is a nicely styled vignette. Landings and hallways are often overlooked spaces because we are usually just passing through. With the addition of an ornate wooden chest and some ethnic artefacts gathered on her travels, this homeowner has turned a dead space into a mini gallery.

art and treasured bits. Think of each group as a collection, and assemble a selection of items of varying height and size, avoiding lining things up too neatly. There are no rules about what should be styled together, but it sometimes helps if there is a common thread or theme that links them together, such as nature, or shades of pink or metallics. A curious little tip that sometimes helps is that groups of odd numbers tend to look better than even. Strange but true!

This is what I call anti-styling, and I approve of it wholeheartedly. For me, bookshelves are best left alone. When you start adding carefully chosen knick-knacks and styling them perfectly, you are much less likely to pick up a book. Books are for reading, not styling.

Creativity before consumption

This has been my mantra for many years, maybe my whole life. I was brought up by a mother who was raised in post-World War II London, so money-saving idioms were rife in our house — a trickle-down effect from my maternal grandmother's own experience with scarcity during the war: 'waste not want not', 'a penny saved is a penny earned' and so on. So yes, this chapter is partly about saving money. However, perhaps more importantly, it is also about originality, because the payoff for being creative is that you often end up with something truly unique.

RIGHT In the Dutch workshop/office of a furniture designer and his team, a huge desk was built from black painted bricks topped with a curved piece of wood. In an opening at one end, a potted tree grows. With some imagination, a version of this could be made with a variety of materials, most of which are easily sourced and inexpensive.

OPPOSITE ABOVE LEFT This simple idea caught my eye. Forget curtain hooks and drape a piece of sheer fabric over a curtain pole. Done. To prevent it slipping, stick it to the pole with double-sided tape.

OPPOSITE ABOVE RIGHT This designer stained plywood, then lined their bedroom walls with it, to give the effect of rusted steel without the expense.

OPPOSITE BELOW LEFT An old weathered ladder is propped beside the bathtub and used as a towel rail. Old ladders are easy to find at antiques markets and are useful in all sizes.

OPPOSITE BELOW RIGHT The most basic of doorstops and perfect in a bohemian home — rocks. You can leave them as they are or paint on a simple geometric pattern.

ABOVE LEFT Rather than buy another bookshelf, this family have used an out-of-use doorway alcove, stacking books and magazines in teetering piles.

ABOVE RIGHT We lost the hardware to my son's bunk beds when we moved house. Instead of buying a new bed, we used part of the bunk frame and fixed it to the top of two Ikea chests of drawers, for a space-saving solution with the added bonus of a secret hideaway underneath.

THERE IS NOTHING WRONG with spending money on something that you love, and this chapter certainly isn't about being frugal for the sake of it. But when you take money out of the equation, and you actually have to use your brain, not your bank account, to solve a problem, brilliant things can happen. Necessity really is the mother of invention. I saw some inspiring examples of creativity when I travelled for this book. For some, it really was a case of necessity: an art student converting a warehouse space with very little cash came up with ingenious uses for salvaged scrapwood – from suspended plant shelves to chairs (see pages 62–67). For others, it was more for the challenge of creating something original: plywood walls were stained to mimic rusted steel for a finish that you can't buy in the shops and one that looks luxe when in fact it was dirt cheap (see page 81).

For me, originality has always been important. I've never wanted to be the same as anyone else, whether in terms of fashion or interiors. I've never coveted designer items, whether a handbag or a sofa (except perhaps my 13-year-old self longing for a pair of green Doc Martens) and always preferred to seek out my own version or customize something store-bought to make it unique. As I get older, my tastes are changing and I've got my eye on a few special pieces, having outgrown the upcycled look. But on my journey for this book, I've been reminded that you can still be a creative maker without sacrificing high style.

TOP LEFT In this warehouse home, there isn't much that isn't fashioned from scrap wood, including this hanging plant shelf. A wooden plank plus rope, and you're done. Paint the wood and use brightly coloured rope for a more playful look.

TOP CENTRE An organic wall hanging was made by the homeowner from shells and pebbles found on the beaches of Morocco. Threaded and knotted onto string, it is a project that's easily adapted to other found objects that catch your eye.

TOP RIGHT The designer who lives here loves plants but is on a budget, so he thinks creatively when looking for plant containers. Buckets, bottles, old jars – anything with sides will do.

ABOVE LEFT I see these big oil drums discarded by restaurants all the time, and they make good plant pots, either left as they are or painted. However, handle with caution – the edges will be sharp and in need of filing down.

ABOVE CENTRE In this kitchen, everything is either handmade or found. The kitchen cabinets utilize old drawers that have been stained black to match the cabinet fronts. Other drawers have been wall hung and are used to store spices.

ABOVE RIGHT In this simple white bathroom, inexpensive peel-and-stick adhesive tiles were added to conceal an unsightly section of the bathroom wall.

BELOW In an old garage in Holland, an entire wall of salvaged doors and windows was built to create valuable storage and display space for this family's many collections. If you prefer a slicker finish, you could paint them all the same colour.

Many of the houses shown in this book are filled with pieces that no one else has. When you look around a space and don't see anything you recognize from any of the big brands, it is refreshing and inspiring. Creativity before consumption isn't just about making the most of what you have, it's also about seeking out raw materials that can be used in interesting ways. A pile of bricks painted black and topped with a slice of tree trunk can become a desk, copper piping makes a simple and effective hanging coat rail and cardboard and paper can be fashioned into pendant lights so cool that I can't stop thinking about them. I urge you to give your creativity a chance before you whip out your credit card.

ABOVE This is such a simple yet brilliant solution for an entryway without anywhere to hang coats. A length of thin copper piping has been threaded with strong twine and hung from eye-hooks in the ceiling to create an instant coat rail.

OPPOSITE This family in Belgium has used inexpensive plywood in so many creative ways. Here, an entire wall of it has a huge impact in the kids' bedroom. They also created a frame for the bunk beds by tying together a handful of long bamboo poles.

THE HOMES

A huge wall (above) divides the central hall from the kitchen in this converted garage. Designed by Piet Hein Eek and made entirely of salvaged doors and windows, it houses the family's many prized collections. In the kitchen (opposite and above), a vintage conference table has been given a new life as a dining table, surrounded by an eclectic group of chairs, stools and sofas. Three shining copper pendant lights tie the space together and bring it a modern edge.

Once a derelict garage, this vast building has been converted into both a home and office space for designers Petra Janssen and Edwin Vollebergh, owners of graphic design agency Studio Boot. Having seen the 'before' pictures, I can tell you that the transformation is mind-blowing. What was once a dank and dirty mess is now a light-filled family home and creative hub.

Retro bohemian

LOCATED ON A QUIET STREET in the centre of Dutch city 's-Hertogenbosch, this unusual building has been cleverly transformed into what Petra calls a 'total concept': a place where the couple and their sons, aged 15 and 17, can 'work, live, eat, listen, love…'.

When Petra and Edwin bought their home four years ago, it was in a terrible state of neglect. Originally built in the 1920s as a factory, it was later used as a car mechanic's garage, then lay empty for 20 years. The building was boarded up and covered in graffiti, and trees had taken

LEFT Paper pendants and antique metal lights add a sense of fun to this already playful interior. This view gives you a sense of the scale and openness of this very unusual home. The wall of doors and windows can be seen below.

BELOW With the clever placement of a group of plants and a day bed, the impression of separate rooms has been created in this open-plan space. An oversized wire floor lamp mirrors the yellow of the painted unit behind.

up clever ideas for the likes of Nike and Coca-Cola, who are among Studio Boot's diverse clientele.

Beyond this is the very heart of the interior, with views all the way up to the three-storey-high roof, made entirely of glass. This large open area has polished concrete floors, a ping pong table at one end and a long table surrounded by chairs at the other. In the middle is a beautiful vintage rug in shades of pink and blue, a contrast to the hard floor. A versatile space that links the 'business' side and the 'family' side of the interior, this hall plays host to meetings and exhibitions, as well as being a recreation area for the

root inside. The couple purchased it with the intention of tearing it down and building something new. However, upon reflection, they decided it would be a shame to demolish it and vowed to rebuild the place, keeping as many of its original features as possible and reusing whatever materials they could.

With its grey painted brick façade, red tiled roof and symmetrical picture windows, the exterior has a charm that belies its size, for this is not a cute cottage but a vast building. Below a tiled sign that reads 'Garage', two large grey doors open onto an entrance space. Immediately to the left and right are two glass cubes, which house the design agency. In these rooms within a room, young creatives tap away on their laptops, presumably dreaming

THIS PAGE Located on the upper floor, overlooking the central enclosed courtyard, this is one of at least four seating areas in the home. Light floods in from the glass roof, highlighting the brightly painted unit. Hiding behind the cheery yellow paint are the utility pipes from the kitchen below. What could have been unsightly has been cleverly disguised and made into a striking feature.

THIS PAGE The owners' love of vintage can be seen in full technicolour here, with the striking mix of a vintage sofa, chair and rug. Convex mirrors, a glittering disco ball and a paper ornament hang from the ceiling, creating a festive vibe. The pop of aqua on the walls and the glimmer of copper in the form of a floor spotlight make this boho room shine.

couple's two teenage sons Piet and Jan: roll up the rug and the expanse of floor is perfect for a spot of skateboarding and bike riding.

The lofty, cathedral-like central space is divided from the back of the building by a vast wall constructed entirely from old, reclaimed doors and windows and stretching the entire width of the building. Designed and built by designer friend Piet Hein Eek, it is an impressive feat of grand proportions. Not only does it make use of a great many salvaged items but it also houses the many collections gathered by Petra and Edwin during their 27 years together. For them this home, and in particular this wall, finally gives them the opportunity to put everything out on display.

On the other side of the wall is the kitchen, which manages to be cosy despite its size. Exposed brick walls, vintage furnishings and shiny copper lights bring warmth and texture to the space, while huge glass and metal doors open on to the garden, where the family's two chickens roam. A staircase leads up to the mezzanine level, which overlooks the central hall below. Here, Petra and Edwin have carved out four bedrooms and furnished them with a mix of vintage and contemporary pieces.

Despite there being very little that is new in this home, the overall effect is of a fresh, modern space. It is eclectic and bohemian, but the pops of colour and the styling throughout prevent it from feeling too kitsch.

ABOVE LEFT A retro chair sits alongside two antique cabinets, while an exciting clash of patterned textiles covers the floor. What keeps the look modern is the barely there pale pink walls, grey trim and bold red vase.

ABOVE RIGHT A seemingly random collection of furniture and textiles makes its own kind of sense when grouped together. The common thread tying the many colours and patterns together is the shot of blue. The simple copper light adds a touch of glam to the painted wall.

OPPOSITE In the large, open live–work space on the ground floor, this decorative wall panel, designed by Petra and Edwin, serves to cleverly conceal rows of shelves behind.

ABOVE This room is where the owners keep some of their prized collections. The workstation was created by building a deep floating shelf between two built-in cupboards. An organic hotchpotch of family photos and memorabilia fills the wall above.

ABOVE RIGHT This ornate armoire is a surprising contrast to the pink corduroy armchair. The stool has been customized with bright yarn strung between the lower rungs and woven over the seat cushion in a geometric pattern.

RIGHT An oversized lampshade and quirky plastic floor light give an injection of modernity to a tranquil bedroom. Keeping the lighting strong in silhouette but neutral in palette allows the vibrant bed cover and blue wall to draw the eye.

THIS PAGE On paper, this combination of colours, styles and shapes shouldn't work, but somehow it does. The retro blue leather 'hands' sofa looks even more striking when paired with a faded vintage rug and a floral cushion. With the addition of the bold artwork, painted by an artist friend, the sofa is elevated from being something of a gimmick to just plain cool.

OPPOSITE Sitting high in the rafters, the master suite is one long, open room. The bed is sandwiched between a bathroom suite (behind the Chinese-style screen) and a dressing room. By restricting the colour palette to orange and yellow, the couple were able to mix various patterns and textures while maintaining a sense of calm in the space.

LEFT The palette here is neutral, just pure white and bare wood, but it has so much character. The lights, the metal table legs, the chairs and even the boat suspended from the ceiling were all made by Bobby.

RIGHT More of Bobby's own designs. The plant box is made from scrap wood and vines clamber up lengths of wire attached with bulldog clips. The blue enamelled cast-iron stool is one of my favourites and is a new venture for Bobby and his design partner.

Handmade home

In a rundown Victorian warehouse in a shabby, industrial part of North London, Swedish product designer Bobby Petersen has created an oasis of calm and creativity on an almost non-existent budget. What was once a dingy, graffiti-riddled space is now a bright, inspiring home bursting with innovative and stylish money-saving ideas and brought to life with plants.

'WASTE NOT, WANT NOT', 'One man's junk is another man's treasure', 'Creativity before consumption'. All these phrases leap to mind when describing Bobby Petersen's home. When Bobby first moved into this rented unit in an as-yet ungentrified warehouse, it was rough around the edges to say the least. He managed to transform the space by working on it in the evenings while studying for an MA at the Royal College of Art during the day. Living on a student budget meant that the renovations were done on the cheap and Bobby's total expenditure was minimal, thanks to his use of salvaged wood and anything else he could get for free.

First, Bobby painted the floors and walls white to cover the graffiti and replaced one set of windows so that he could open them. He then set about constructing two loft rooms that made full use of the unit's double-height ceiling. It took a month to build the rooms, one of which Bobby sleeps in. For privacy, he designed a flap door that can be raised

and lowered by the use of a pulley and concrete counterweight. Beneath the bedroom is a workshop area, where Bobby keeps tools and supplies; on the other side is the kitchen, with open shelves and everything on display. Above, a small mezzanine leads to the second loft room. With shelves, a desk and a chair – all made by Bobby – it is a tiny office high up in the rafters (and not for the faint of heart).

OPPOSITE A steep ladder leads up to the tiny mezzanine above the kitchen. One of Bobby's Musical Chairs plus a simple piece of wood for a desk turn this vertiginous spot into a home office. The red door leads to one of the small bedrooms.

LEFT Good use is made of the windowsills, which are home to plants at various stages of growth. Bottles, tins and buckets have all been turned into makeshift plant pots.

ABOVE I love Bobby's pendant lights, handmade from cardboard and rice paper, and hung amidst the jungle-like greenery.

There is very little in his home that has not been devised and made by Bobby himself, from chairs to table legs to pendant lights. He says he is interested in 'adapting design by altering an object's use', and his designs include the 'Paper Pulp Helmet'; a bike helmet made from discarded newspapers; an interactive installation called Musical Chairs, which allowed museum-goers to make their own music by sitting on his note-playing chairs made from scrap wood (it was exhibited at the Victoria and Albert Museum when Bobby was still a student); and a single-passenger boat driven and navigated by a smartphone and built-in GPS. The chairs and boat are now part of the flat's décor, the boat hanging from the rafters in the living room and the chairs dotted all around.

Having grown up surrounded by nature in Sweden, Bobby has cultivated his love of plants in his urban loft. Passion flower vines grow in scrapwood boxes; a plank hanging from the ceiling makes a platform for potted plants; windowsills are lined with containers of all kinds – soup tins, plastic drink bottles – each holding a seed, a bulb or a cutting.

There is little pattern or colour here, except for the powder blue interior of the bedroom flap door, but the effect is far from bland. Evidence of the handmade is everywhere, giving the home texture and soul. Everything here has a story; whether it was part of an installation, a university project or made out of necessity, it has a reason for being.

ABOVE Adding two rooms to the high-ceilinged warehouse gave Bobby much more space, not just for living but also to store his belongings. The outer walls of the loft rooms have been put to good use: one supports storage boxes on brackets and the other displays his Musical Chairs installation.

OPPOSITE Above the sofa, a sheet of tarnished metal becomes art. It was a test for the metal side tables that Bobby designed with his studio partner Tom Gottelier, and is an industrial material not typically used for domestic objects, despite its inherent beauty.

ABOVE Custom-built metal folding doors open onto the shaded courtyard. A fast-growing pepper tree is a great way to add natural shade in a hurry – this one grew from a seedling to its current height in just four years.

RIGHT At the top of the stairs, a classic Eames rocker, a vintage lamp, and a collection of carved wooden objects unite to fill an often neglected space – the upstairs landing.

OPPOSITE The social hub of this home is the kitchen; a cool blend of trad Moroccan and 1960s styling. Ceramic pendant lights hang over the central island, while vintage art and colourful tagines decorate the shelves behind. Acrylic bar stools and a vintage rug tie in with the dominant colour story of orange, red and yellow.

Bright barn

Former florist Emma Wilson left her flower stall in London's Knightsbridge for a three-day trip to Essaouira. When she returned, she had bought a house in the picturesque Moroccan seaside town. Sixteen years and a couple of houses later, the British expat is settled here in Sidi Kaouki, where she converted this 70-year-old barn into the stunning home it is today. Emma has deftly mixed smooth concrete floors with vintage Moroccan rugs and retro furniture from London's Brick Lane for an effect that is part Moorish, part space age and all boho modern.

THIS IS THE THIRD AND MOST RECENT house Emma Wilson has bought in Morocco, and she has lived in this one for four years now. What started on a whim many years ago has become a flourishing business, Castles in the Sand, which sees her renting out her two former homes to holidaymakers from all over the world and as a location for photo shoots (see pages 124–131). Emma also runs Beldi Rugs, a company specializing in authentic Moroccan Berber rugs. Her home doubles as a showroom, with a stunning collection of rugs on display in every room.

Emma lives with her son Kai and a trio of pets – cats Ziggy Blue and Whiskas and dog Chica – all of whom seem to lead a blessed life in this colourful home. Emma has

done a huge amount of work to get the home to its current state. She retained the three main stone walls and rebuilt the remainder with typical Moroccan architecture in mind – wooden beams, thick stone walls and a central courtyard. From the outside the house appears entirely conventional: a whitewashed box covered with bougainvillea and accessed via a bumpy road leading to the sea. But step inside and it is far from traditional.

Emma and her ex-partner Graham Carter, with whom she moved to Morocco, once owned interiors shops in London, specializing in vintage furniture. Her Moroccan homes are filled with vintage pieces collected over the years and the retro influence is obvious, with pieces from the 1960s and '70s throughout.

The front door leads directly into a single large room that encompasses the living, cooking and dining areas. Sunlight streams in through specially designed metal doors that lead onto a courtyard. It doesn't feel cluttered, like some open-plan homes can, but neither is it minimalist. Emma has designed her home to provide a blank canvas against which her colourful collections can enjoy pride of place. The floor and surfaces are made from *tadelakt*, a traditional Moroccan lime plaster finish used

OPPOSITE The table and benches were custom-made with metal legs to counter a puppy's chewing habit – look closely and you will see 'Milly Proof' embossed on the metal. The wood-beamed ceiling and vibrant art by Dan Baldwin add warmth and character to this modern interior.

ABOVE A 1970s leather corner sofa by de Sede creates a cosy seating area in this open-plan room. Colourful patterned cushions, a vintage Moroccan rug and a mid-century coffee table bring just the right amount of eclectic to the clean white walls and concrete floors.

RIGHT In the centre of the open-plan living space sits an enormous chimney breast. Polished concrete can feel hard or cold, but Emma has given the chimney a bit of soul in the form of a hessian firewood bag and the collection of wooden trinkets, which are in fact parts of an old loom.

THIS PAGE With the addition of a desk and chair, this small space on the first floor has become a quiet work area away from the bustle of downstairs. It also makes a good spot for Emma's collection of framed family photos, hung from floor to ceiling in a charmingly haphazard style.

in the hammams of Morocco. Paired with the whitewashed walls, this neutral but textural backdrop allows the vibrant Berber rugs and pops of colour to sing out. Along one wall is the kitchen, Emma's favourite part of the home. Separated from the living area by a long *tadelakt* island, it is filled with a bright and eclectic mix of pots and other kitchenwares.

In the centre of the room is a huge open fireplace, made from – you guessed it – *tadelakt*. This is the heart of the home, a warming centre around which to gather. To the left is a generous seating area, with a large leather sofa and a smattering of patterned pillows. To the right, close to the metal doors, is a custom-built dining table and benches, a lovely spot to eat, work or play.

Open-plan living isn't for everyone; it requires a certain amount of effort and discipline to keep everything looking streamlined and shipshape. Care should also be taken when choosing a colour palette. Pieces in the living space need to sit well with the contents of the kitchen area and so on. There's nothing wrong with an eclectic look, but it helps to tie it together with a shared group of colours, something Emma demonstrates so perfectly in her stylish home.

ABOVE LEFT AND RIGHT
In Kai's bedroom, these built-in shelves are both organic and modern, like a futuristic cave. With perfectly unstyled 'kid-mess' on display, they come to life. The pressure of a tidy room hinders creativity in some kids – let there be mess! Opposite are the clean-lined bunk beds, with bright blue bed linen that's echoed in the diptych of a grinning whale. Emma's vintage rug and Nigerian beaded armchair add a quirky touch.

ABOVE In Emma's bedroom, she designed a platform for her bed that incorporates shelves on either side for books, lamps and the usual bits and pieces. She has warmed up the neutral palette with a patterned quilt and bold painting by artist Dan Baldwin.

ABOVE RIGHT On the other side of the bedroom is a contemporary chaise longue and graphic curtains. The moulded fibreglass shelves are a vintage find and offer a clean display platform for a collection of wooden and beaded pieces.

RIGHT The entrance from the master bedroom to its en suite bathroom is via a rounded cut-out in the wall. Here again Emma has used a rug to add colour and texture. There is no rule that says only bath mats belong in bathrooms!

OPPOSITE The master bathroom is a warm cocoon of a room, finished entirely in *tadelakt*, a traditional Moroccan lime plaster finish that's deliciously soft underfoot. The bathtub is the only contemporary piece, and contrasts beautifully with the wooden stool and beaded wall art.

Bohemian grandeur

When I heard about a couple who owned a café and B&B called *Le Jardin Bohémien*, I thought it might be a good fit for this book. My French is limited, but I knew that it translated to The Bohemian Garden, something I liked the sound of. But nothing could have prepared me for this sprawling, brilliantly decorated home and business in the Belgian city of Ghent. Set over three floors in an 18th-century townhouse just steps from the canal, Jeanpierre Detaeye and Kristine Dehond have created a home so stylish and creative that it almost defies words.

I HAD A MAJOR CASE OF HOUSE/LIFE ENVY when I stepped inside, first into the huge café on the ground floor, then up the dramatic staircase into the home of Jeanpierre, an interior designer, and Kristine, a sculptor. The café itself is big and eclectic. It mixes old and new, taxidermy and plywood, neon pink and peeling paint for a style that resists categorization. As well as being a cool place for coffee and cake, everything in the café is for sale – because why not?

Jeanpierre and Kristine occupy the two upper floors with their sons – Emile, ten, and Jerome, eight – sweet, long-haired boys who play with Lego and handmade wooden toys for hours on end (no video games here).

THIS PAGE In the living room, a Hans Wegner AP 16 leather chair with a beautiful patina nestles next to a tiny bamboo armchair. The metal shelf holds an impressive collection of glassware, including some 1960s Holmegaard vases, a gleaming contrast to the wood furniture.

From the café, an imposing, curved staircase leads upwards to their quarters and the B&B, passing a taxidermy stag and an 18th-century fresco on the way. At the top of the stairs is a large landing, spacious enough to house Jeanpierre's office. A door leads straight into the B&B, a huge room with large windows and white-painted floorboards that feels modern and stylish. The bed has a simple, boxy plywood frame, the bold grain its only embellishment. The walls closest to the bed are also clad in sheets of plywood, precisely incised with a grid pattern. The plywood theme is repeated elsewhere in the room, my favourite use being to frame the television set, which has been inset into the fireplace.

Back on the landing, a door leads to the family's living quarters: kitchen, dining and living. The rooms are large, the ceilings high and the floorboards creak in a comforting fashion that reminds you that you are in a very old house. Whereas the café and B&B have a 21st-century quirkiness to them, the family home is more mature and sophisticated. The colour palette is rich and jewel-like and the furnishings are a glamorous, decadent mix of vintage and classic designer pieces, most with endearing signs of wear.

On the very top floor are the family bedrooms. Jeanpierre and Kristine's room is dark and serene, with two walls clad in lauan plywood stained to resemble Cor-Ten steel, like a Richard Serra sculpture. To offset the darkness, one wall is painted a rich pink and the bedspread is white with large black polka dots. In the room shared by the boys, a plain bunk bed has been screened off by gauzy white cotton, attached to a makeshift bamboo frame. Except for a red rug and a red bedspread, the room is

ABOVE LEFT In a corner of the family living room, the boys' toy castles blend in with classic vintage furniture and lighting. You can see the scale of the room from the size of the door behind the shelving unit.

LEFT In *Le Jardin Bohémien*, the café that Jeanpierre and Kristine run on the ground floor of their home, an eclectic mix of furniture makes for a cosy, 'hanging out at home' atmosphere. The red pendant lights are ceramic and the neon pink shelf is handmade from plywood.

RIGHT Kristine is currently using the dining room as an office space, so computer and printer cables are inevitable. Embrace this fact of modern life and choose cables in bright colours – if they can't be hidden, then make them stand out.

RIGHT In the family's B&B, an entire corner of the room has been clad in plywood, expertly cut with a grid pattern. In the fireplace, the television is turned into a feature by giving it a plywood frame. The blue backing that surrounds it is actually a type of drywall sheeting that was deliberately left unpainted by Jeanpierre, who liked the finish.

BELOW On a wall in the B&B, an oval of brick was intentionally left exposed when the wall was replastered, creating a quirky unexpected feature.

earthy and natural, with sheepskins, cow hide rugs and a huge animal skull hanging on the wall. Even their toys are natural (except for the ubiquitous Lego); every corner has a basket of wooden bows and swords.

There is an authenticity to this home that resonates. Although designer furniture is in abundance, its worn condition signals that the pieces have been well loved, not just put on display as status symbols. Kristine's work has taken over the dining room table and tangled computer wires trail across the floor. Thanks to the lived-in furniture

and the overflowing bookshelves, the boys' Lego and the computer cables on the floor, this feels like a real home and makes a refreshing change from the images of perfect homes that we are bombarded with in blogs and magazines. Given that I'm a stylist, this may sound strange – after all, part of my job is to make homes look perfect. But a home can still be beautiful with real-life bits and pieces on display. In fact, as I write this, there are computer wires snaking across my own kitchen floor. Life is messy. And in this townhouse in Ghent, it is also very, very beautiful.

RIGHT In the master bedroom, the wall behind the bed was clad in lauan plywood and stained to resemble the rusty finish of Cor-Ten steel, a favourite material of sculptor Richard Serra. A classic bentwood chair by Thonet sits against the eye-popping pink wall, and the door is being tested for a coat of pink paint as well. Round wooden knobs by Muuto hold an assortment of Kristine's necklaces.

OPPOSITE In the boys' bedroom, Kristine has made a bamboo frame to surround the bunk beds, from which she has hung white fabric that instantly creates a fort-like vibe in the already outdoorsy room. The boys have a little mattress that they spill their Lego onto so that they can move their creations around the room.

ABOVE From the main landing there is access to a spacious roof garden. The exterior walls have been refinished in a modern grey plaster, but are softened by the addition of lemon trees and cacti.

ABOVE RIGHT Opposite the boys' bunk bed is a single bed covered in a thick wool blanket. A classic Eames rocker is made cosier with an extra-thick sheepskin. The ladder is fixed to the wall – my guess is that the boys leap from it onto the bed.

RIGHT The desk's blue metal legs and the blue lamp play nicely against the natural elements in the rest of the boys' bedroom.

The greenhouse

Dorthe Kvist is a garden designer and author of two gardening books. She shares her charming, plant-filled home with husband Jakob and their two children Otto, 11, and Ella, 6. Built in 1937 on a tree-lined street a short cycle ride from central Copenhagen, their home exudes a sense of warmth and love. Whitewashed wooden floors and dappled light from the lime tree outside provide a calming backdrop for an unpretentious mix of classic Scandinavian furniture, Moroccan rugs and 'granny chic' sofas. But what takes it to the next level is the abundance of plants – this home is literally alive with greenery.

OPPOSITE Just off the living room is the family dining area, which sits within the open-plan kitchen. A set of classic chairs is paired with a vintage wooden table, and above hangs a trio of industrial-style pendant lights. Alone, these pieces could feel a little stark, but with the addition of a potted tree and a colour-blocked shelf of cookbooks, the space is immediately warmed up.

ABOVE A row of tiles left over from a project provides a unique centrepiece on the dining table. A rotating display of small plants and cuttings are arranged in miniature bottles picked up by Dorthe at antiques markets and junk shops.

BELOW At the top of the stairs, a cane bench and a cowhide rug create a spot for relaxation on a landing that would have been wasted space. Wooden coathooks by Muuto and shelves that house an overflow of shoes turn this into a practical and pretty spot.

FROM THE MOMENT YOU WALK through the door, you know this is a happy home. It is bright, airy and cheerful, and you get the sense that nothing is for show; everything serves a purpose or is truly loved. Dorthe's decorating philosophy is simple: 'Whatever makes you happiest'. She doesn't subscribe to the notion that a home should look like those on the glossy pages of a magazine, even though hers does. Instead, Dorthe sees her home and garden as a workshop, a playground and a laboratory – somewhere to have fun and experiment with new ideas.

What matters to Dorthe and her family is that their home is filled with things that tell a story. So there are rugs from a trip to Marrakech, ceramics from Greece, wooden chopping boards from France, a Buddha from Vietnam and cushions from Bangkok. Dorthe's bohemian spirit is evident in these pieces and the memories they hold for her. However, she isn't opposed to mixing in a bit of Ikea. Nor is she above a bit of 'dumpster diving', as they sometimes call it in the States. Finding discarded bits of furniture at her local bulky waste drop-off gives her great pleasure, and she loves the feeling of recycling something that was destined for landfill.

When Dorthe and Jakob bought their house, it was in a terrible state. Dorthe oversaw the renovation while on maternity leave with newborn Ella, the baby in her arms. Six years on, it is a glowing example of great light, smart design and the one thing you can't fake:

ABOVE In the living room, Dorthe has created a vignette that is both practical and interesting. The shelving unit is made of industrial piping and flanges and parts of old crates. It is softened by the Moroccan rug, the delicate plants and the grouping of vintage glass.

LEFT Dorthe loves cane benches. This one is layered with a soft cotton rug and positioned in front of a bold floral painting. The yellow leather Moroccan pouffe picks out the yellow in the painting, tying the whole look together.

THIS PAGE Never underestimate the power of a restricted colour palette. Black, white, wood and a pop of yellow make this room sing. A framed poster, shapely vases and even quirky speakers are elevated to the status of 'a collection' when they share a colour theme. The sleek Danish cabinet and the large branch add warmth to the room.

a good eye. It comes as no surprise to discover that an avid gardener lives here. Aside from a few splashes of bold colour dotted here and there, the main accent shade throughout is green, as in glossy, lush leaves.

Dorthe is so passionate about plants that it's hard to imagine her doing anything else, but before becoming a garden designer she was a fashion designer, travelling the globe and seeking the next big trend in the fast-paced world of fashion. It seems that her home now is a reflection of the calm she has found since leaving the fashion industry for garden design, a career that allows her to create something with a longer lifespan than fashion's three-month cycle.

The ground floor consists of an open-plan living space – two rooms knocked into one – with two distinct seating areas and a dining room that leads onto the kitchen. The palette throughout is calm, clean and neutral: white walls, white cotton blinds and bleached floorboards. Furniture is kept simple and natural too, but still has personality. There is nothing too loud or attention-seeking – except perhaps the bright yellow Moroccan pouffes – and nothing too self-conscious in the way the space is curated. In the more formal of the two seating areas, a floral sofa and armchair live harmoniously with a yellow-legged, marble-topped coffee

OPPOSITE **The boxy shapes of these floral sofas and their pairing with vintage cane chairs and Moroccan rugs prevent this space from feeling old-fashioned. The yellow pop of colour is carried over from the connecting room and can be seen in the metal legs of the coffee table and the little pouffe beyond. A vintage print of a greenhouse and a shapely black cardboard pendant inject just the right amount of quirkiness and contrast.**

ABOVE RIGHT AND RIGHT **Plants and natural elements are the main attraction in this home. They occupy every table and windowsill, and even hang from the ceiling. Here, concrete pots are suspended in neon macramé holders made by Dorthe. Next to them is a collection of prints, printed onto plain paper and taped to the wall (above right). A lesson to remember: art doesn't have to be complicated or expensive to look good.**

table, vintage cane chairs and Moroccan rugs. Somehow it all works. Because the palette is soft, nothing fights for attention. The floral sofas and the cane chairs look as if they would be perfectly at home in the conservatory of an elderly lady who loves a bit of chintz with her afternoon tea and cake. But when paired with a sculptural black pendant light and concrete planters suspended in neon macramé, they create an entirely different look. Set all this against a lush backdrop of potted plants, and it's a bit like living in a greenhouse. I'm sure that was no accident.

The rest of the home exudes the same sense of calm, but with a dash more colour and pattern here and there. Dorthe and Jakob's home feels relaxed and effortless, with just the right balance of bohemian and modern elements so as not to feel overwhelming.

ABOVE In the master bedroom, there is a sense of sophistication in the buttoned headboard and the luscious linens. Dorthe has expertly layered in colour and texture in the form of the Moroccan rugs and the paper pompoms dangling above the bed. The black metal lights bring a modern edge.

RIGHT In Ella's bedroom, a small bed is slotted cosily between the wall and a painted wooden beam. The rug and bedcover share a similar colour palette of pinks and blues, and add punchiness to the white walls. The yellow Perspex chair and blue lava lamp give it a jolt of perfect Bohemian Modern styling.

OPPOSITE On a deck outside the kitchen/dining room, a seating area has been built from pallets and old sofa cushions covered in linen. Dorthe also made the tie-dye cushions and the tree stump tables, cleverly set on wheels for easy mobility. Beyond is the garden shed, with vegetable boxes built onto the roof.

Technicolour home

In a 19th-century factory building in The Netherlands, a textile designer and her family have created a colourful and eclectic haven in the midst of a city centre. Filled with West African textiles, vibrant-hued walls and treasures from around the world, it is a feast for the eyes and a lesson in artfully blending old with new.

RIGHT AND OPPOSITE The view from the kitchen into the dining room reveals what an inviting space it is. The room was an addition by a former owner and feels like an extension of the back garden. The lanterns were found in NYC's Chinatown and are hung in a cluster above the table.

AS COLOURFUL AS THIS LIVELY HOME IS, Kim Schipperheijn assures me that it is calmer than it once was. Kim and her partner Homme-Auke Kooistra moved into this apartment in the city of Nijmegen four years ago and it has been through a few changes before settling into its current Bohemian Modern incarnation. Where there were once 'hippy wallpapers, flowery curtains and granny carpets,' now there is a sophisticated fusion of colour and pattern. The family has also doubled in size since they

moved in, with the birth of daughters Sientje, aged two, and Doris, just two months old.

The apartment is in a building that dates back to 1880 and was once a carpentry factory. The original features are still in place, including the mouldings on the 13-foot/4-metre-high ceilings and the beautiful, wide floorboards, which have been painted grey. The walls in the living room and kitchen are bright white but all the other rooms have been painted in a cheery combination of colours,

THIS PAGE The living room benefits from dramatic high ceilings and original architectural features. Above the fireplace, a piece of Vlisco fabric has been stretched over a canvas to create a quick, easy and inexpensive piece of art. The clean-lined, boxy green sofa is the Polder by Dutch designer Hella Jongerius.

from mustard to aqua to papaya pink. Against the traditional architectural detailing of the building, the mismatched colours work well together to create a fresh, modern vibe.

Kim works as a designer for Dutch textiles brand Vlisco, who manufacture elaborately patterned fashion fabrics mainly for the West African market. She has incorporated some Vlisco fabrics into her décor, covering a sofa in one print, stretching another on canvas like art and using a third as a bedcover. The fabrics are just one of many global influences here: the lanterns over the dining area were picked up in New York's Chinatown, the portraits on the dining room wall were all collected on various trips to Indonesia, where Kim was born, and the carved wooden statue on the mantelpiece was brought back from the Caribbean by Kim's father; there are also paintings from Congo and Benin.

LEFT In the papaya pink dining room, a glossy black piano is decked out with family treasures, including one of Kim's collection of dog statues and a mask from Mexico. Beyond the dining/music room is the children's room, with its aqua walls. Shades of pink, red, and blue give this corner a cohesive look.

ABOVE In the living room, a section of wall has been turned into a gallery space. Even the playpen mattress has been given an update with a cheerful patterned fabric. The yellow-painted clock case divides the wall and creates definition in the open-plan space. The pair of armchairs just beyond were reupholstered by Kim's mother using old knitted jumpers.

In the girls' bedroom, Kim opted for an intense aqua blue shade on the walls. Despite the bright hue, the room still feels serene. A glossy green set of drawers is used as a changing table and the small striped bag hides baby wipes (below right). A collection of painted wooden dolls – one in need of repair – hang in a neat row on the wall (below left).

LEFT Custom-made bunk beds were designed for the girls to share, with removable child gates to keep them safe. Even more colour is layered here – lemon yellow walls inside the bunks and geometric blankets in neon pink. Eclectic handmade touches are needed to break up the solid blocks of vibrant colour: dream-catchers and patterned pillows work well.

The home is essentially a rectangle in shape, stretching from the street to the garden at the rear. The living room is at the front and leads into the kitchen then the dining room, which is housed in a 'garden room' built by the former owner. This space doubles as a music room, where Homme-Auke plays the piano and bass guitar. With doors that open to the lush garden beyond and a warm glow from the pink walls, the room is an inviting hub of activity, from making art and music to eating and drinking around the simple dining table surrounded by vintage chairs.

The bedrooms are situated at the back of the apartment, looking out onto the garden. A large bedroom was divided into two smaller ones to accommodate the growing family. In the girls' bedroom, the couple built bunk beds with removable child gates to keep the little ones safe. Again, they didn't hold back when it comes to colour, mixing apple green with lemon yellow, neon pink and aqua. It seems that Kim and Homme-Auke have never met a colour they didn't like and the result is a warm and happy home that is filled to the brim with personality.

THIS PAGE In the couple's bedroom at the back of the house, they chose mustard yellow for the walls. To add interest, Kim dipped into her collection of fabrics to cover the bed.

THIS PAGE In the large kitchen, a shaft of sunlight streams from above onto the softly patterned tile floor. A bare bulb hangs in front of the built-in cabinets, held in a decorative metal clasp.

OPPOSITE ABOVE The inner courtyard follows the Moroccan tradition of a riad having a fountain and four orange or lemon trees. The central pool has a cooling effect on the home and, of course, looks beautiful.

Deep within the confines of the medina in Marrakech, behind a glossy black door set within a dusty wall, is the home of designer Agnes Emery of Emery & Cie, a Brussels-based design house specializing in beautiful collections of tiles, paint, rugs and furniture.

No surface untouched

AS THE ORNATELY ENGRAVED DOOR opens inwards from the dark alley, you are met by a riot of greens and blues, pattern upon pattern, tile beside tile. It is a shock to the senses, so much beauty hidden behind crumbling walls. Like a geode whose rock-like surface gives no hint at the crystals within, so are the riads of Morocco, and Agnes's home is no exception.

Agnes doesn't live here full time and she refers to it as a 'work-house'. Her home is in Brussels, near her studio and showroom, but many of her products are manufactured in Morocco, so she spends a great deal of time here. Agnes offers the house as a holiday getaway to all the members of her team; a very nice perk of the job, I'd say!

ABOVE Only natural products have a place in Agnes's home, even the shopping baskets. Woven in a beautiful concentric circle pattern, this example feels modern and fresh.

Agnes bought the building about ten years ago and hasn't made any major changes apart from updating the plumbing and electrics and redecorating. The structure remains the same: a traditional Moroccan riad complete with four citrus trees and a fountain in the inner courtyard, as is the norm. When Agnes thought of how to decorate her riad, she imagined it would be occupied by parakeets and this informed her design, and particularly the colour palette – vibrant greens and blues are the common thread throughout. Only an imagination like hers – parakeets! – could dream up such a scheme.

A couple of things stand out about this home, aside from how jaw-droppingly gorgeous it is. The first is that there is almost nothing that is new here. Everything appears to have a history and nothing shines in that 'just bought' kind of way. Even the tiles, designed by Agnes and obviously relatively new, have a subtle patina of age. The second thing is that there isn't a surface that has been left untouched. There is no bare wood in sight – ceilings, doors, cupboards and tables have all been painted some exquisite shade of Emery & Cie paint and many have been hand stencilled too. Floors, walls and stairs have

ABOVE AND OPPOSITE BELOW LEFT A tiny nook just off the kitchen offers a cool refuge and a relaxing spot for tea. The acid green paint is a sharp contrast to the traditional shape of the small archway.

OPPOSITE ABOVE LEFT Built-in kitchen cupboards are painted soft dove grey inside and out. Even simple shelves slotted into a niche can become a thing of beauty when tucked behind a curving ogee arch.

OPPOSITE ABOVE RIGHT Agnes has artfully married greens and yellows in the kitchen and has carried the theme over to the collection of bowls on the shelf. Note the pleasingly organic and imperfect manner in which the *zellige* tiles have been laid.

OPPOSITE BELOW RIGHT The use of a warm, matt grey paint on the doors tempers the harshness of the lime green paint on the walls. Adding another bright colour to the mix would have caused too much visual friction.

OPPOSITE This secluded seating area has a luxurious velvet banquette and cushions. Mirrored discs of varying sizes have been set into the plaster around the cupboard. On the floor sits an intricate metal pendant light waiting to be hung.

been covered with a stunning selection of tiles in varying designs. The effect on the eye is extremely satisfying. Despite the wealth of pattern and colour at every turn, the interior flows seamlessly, helped in large part by an unwavering adherence to a colour story of blues and greens.

This home may not have the obvious modern elements seen in some of the others in this book, but for me what makes it modern is Agnes's designs and colours, and, even more so, her dedication to keeping dying crafts alive. In this age of making more, making it quicker, making it cheaper, Agnes pays great attention to the way her products are made

ABOVE LEFT A calming effect is created by the use of tone on tone in this bedroom. Shades of aqua, eau de nil, leaf green and silvery grey are expertly combined in the tiles, table and even the goatskin rug. A dash of modernity and humour is added in the form of two retro alarm clocks.

ABOVE Again, Agnes provides a masterclass in tone-on-tone layering on a stairwell that is open to the elements. The tiles and paint are the same shade of blue as the sky above and will eventually be bleached by the sun, an effect that Agnes welcomes.

ABOVE LEFT Another small work area is hidden away in a room off the blue stairwell. The modern desk lamp is one of only a handful of contemporary pieces in the home.

ABOVE RIGHT A compact but functional workspace has been created by tucking a desk under the stairs.

OPPOSITE Just off the all-blue stairwell is a bedroom, cool and dim, tucked away from the glare of the sun. An example of Agnes's fresco painting can be glimpsed on the wall behind. The mustard-coloured bedspread is from the Emery & Cie archives.

and strives to ensure that those who produce them are well paid – to me, that is an entirely modern way of thinking. Contradictory, I know!

Agnes's design philosophy, roughly translated from the French, is 'to search for perfection in imperfection'. She sees beauty in the uneven and irregular – the slight differences in each of her tiles, evidence of the touch of human hand; or the rough finish of a plastered wall, so much more soulful than a perfectly smooth one.

Clearly, Agnes is someone who tries her hand at many things. Rather than suffer the frustration of struggling to convey what's in her head to someone else, she attempts it herself. Not only does she design many of the patterns for her company's collections but she also paints fresco, applying beautiful scrolling designs onto freshly applied plaster so that her design sets into the plaster as it dries and becomes a permanent part of the wall. Her home seems to be a place for constant experimentation, with many new ideas tried and tested within its boundaries.

THIS PAGE People can become obsessed with sleek and glossy perfection, particularly when it comes to bathrooms. What makes this one so charming is the roughness of the walls and the irregularity of the *zellige* tiles and grout. If everything were lined up perfectly, it would lose its character. The shades of pale green and grey are a soothing choice for a bathroom.

OPPOSITE The riad's rooftop is baking hot, with stunning views of Marrakech. Respite from the relentless sun can be enjoyed in this corner, shaded by a custom-built metal frame and bamboo roof. Here, Agnes has mixed five or six varying designs, all in shades of blue – the perfect example of how to layer pattern on pattern.

Our home for now is a rented Victorian terraced house in North London, decorated in a mix of found furniture, bargain buys and homemade bits and pieces. When we moved in two years ago we had very little, having sold everything when we moved back to London from Los Angeles. In a relatively short time, we have made ourselves a comfortable and eclectic home, using a few stylist's tricks, a little bit of imagination and a lot of 'make do and mend' spirit.

Urban bohemian

ABOVE In my living room, the wall hanging was a hasty afterthought when dip-dyeing the curtains. I had leftover dye, a piece of grey linen and a blank wall.

RIGHT In order to fit the sofa into the living room, we had to block a door with our Chinese armoire. The artwork is by Duncan Simpson, the paper zebra head by Anthropologie and ceramics by a teenage me.

THIS IS NOT MY DREAM HOUSE. I'm sure that I'm not supposed to say that, but it's the truth. I love our home and I can see its potential, but it isn't yet a true reflection of my style. If anything, it's a reflection of our journey over the past few years and, as such, it certainly tells a story. But it's still in its infancy, unlike some of the extraordinary, fully formed homes shown in the rest of the book. Rather, ours is a makeshift home, cobbled together in a period of upheaval in our lives and still evolving.

THIS PAGE A found table, painted grey, sits in the bay window and holds my two favourite things: plants and books. The rug and Florence Balducci pillow are from Anthropologie, the industrial lamp and coffee table from a local shop, Homage. The red chair is a sentimental family piece.

OPPOSITE In the kitchen, I transformed a blank wall into a family gallery, backed with wallpaper scraps. I made some modern macramé in neon string and covered the kitchen chairs with Dutch wax fabric, easily changeable when the mood strikes.

BELOW AND RIGHT The dining room became our office with the addition of a pair of Ikea desks and two found chairs. The aqua wall came with the house and has gradually grown on me. The artwork in white frames is by the LA painter Kim West and my daughter.

Three years ago, I moved my family from my adopted home of Los Angeles back to London, where I was born and raised. My husband Erick is a film editor and we have two children – Ella is 15 and Johnny is 12. I had lived in America for half my life and had accumulated an obscene amount of stuff, even for a magpie-like stylist. Rather than ship it all, we sold or gave away almost all our belongings, except two pieces of furniture. At first, it was liberating – it's just stuff, I told myself – but later, quite traumatic.

Arriving in London, we had two weeks to find a home, schools and, believe it or not, jobs. We are either courageous risk-takers or reckless idiots; the jury is still out. We rushed into one of the first rented flats we found – all beige carpet and cheap furniture. I cried my way through the first year, desperate to tear up the carpets, paint the walls and make it my own. On a weekly basis I announced to my husband – an American thoroughly enjoying living in London – that we should go back to LA.

THIS PAGE Our bedroom is a blank canvas, getting frequent updates through the textiles, most of which are made by me. I also made the wire wall art – a favourite phrase that I try to remember: 'All that now exists was once imagined'. I like how wonky and imperfect the writing looks.

OPPOSITE ABOVE I've tried to add some personality to the beige-painted wardrobes with touches of copper, citrus and black, the inspiration coming from a vintage dress I've had for years. I turned the silver wardrobe handles black with a black/dotty washi tape. Neutral-coloured zipper bags provide additional clothes storage above.

BELOW I found this huge frame and painted it in chalkboard paint. It has moved around the house a lot and is currently a backdrop for all my bits and pieces – necklaces, shoes, bags. I found the chair, painted it white and added fabric to the seat. The dotty pillow is by Madison & Grow.

However, a year later, once we had found our feet, we spotted this three-bedroom house for rent in Stoke Newington, a pretty part of North London with a charming village feel. (To buy property in London these days you either have to be a banker or have a trust fund, neither of which applies to us, so for now we rent.) The house has lovely features, including dark floorboards and ornate fireplaces, and it was empty when we moved in.

We only shipped over two pieces of furniture from LA – a red velvet armchair and a Chinese armoire painted with butterflies. I wouldn't buy the armchair if I saw it now, but it was the very first thing Erick and I bought together more than 15 years ago when we were broke and had a brand-new baby. I nursed my kids in that chair and I can't seem to let it go. It's a similar story with the armoire – it was an early purchase and the only 'grown-up' thing we have ever bought.

Over the last two years, we have pieced together a home in the most frugal fashion imaginable. In the back of my mind, I thought we might move back to LA and I didn't want the wrenching experience of buying

LEFT A favourite vintage dress brightens a window. I will never wear this again (I did once…), but I still like to look at it. I often hang a beautiful piece of clothing on display as though it were art.

BELOW In Johnny's room, his own art, saved over the years, decorates the wall. His bed is a wooden platform placed atop two Ikea chests of drawers. There is a hiding place beneath that's hidden behind a curtain.

OPPOSITE In Ella's room, I was asked to tone down the colours a bit, so the palette is black, white and red only, and even extends to her magazine tears and artwork. I sneaked in some blue in the form of a tie-dyed piece of linen on the bed; a first attempt that sparked the idea for *shibori* dyeing.

stuff, then selling everything again. Instead, I dip-dyed inexpensive, plain curtains, sewed pillows from fabric offcuts, and made wall art from lengths of cheap wire. I've picked up almost every piece of furniture spotted by the side of the road and worked my magic on them. At one point, nearly everything in the house was a 'street find' (not necessarily a good look, I might add…)

I've always been more of a maker than a consumer and have been 'upcycling' since long before it was a word, but I may have reached my limit of thriftiness with this house. There comes a time when you want to buy exactly what you want, and not just make do. Thankfully, after living in a state of limbo for a long time, we decided to put down some roots and buy a few new bits. Our home will continue to evolve, as any good stylist's home should, with ideas being tested and developed until it feels just right. And at about that point, the bohemian wanderer in me will probably tear it all down, move on to another project and start all over again.

OPPOSITE The dining room sits just below the pulpit, one of the original features of the church. The pew behind the table didn't come with the building but seemed the obvious choice for dining room seating. The lighting is a vintage purchase and an interesting choice against the wallpaper.

RIGHT A pair of retro-style metal chairs are the perfect spot for relaxing in the back garden. Maaike likes to sit here and make macramé hanging baskets for plants.

In a little village in the far north of the Netherlands, a window dresser and a nature lover have combined their passions to create a family home in a converted church. Light-filled and thoughtfully curated, this unusual home has a sophistication that one might expect to find in a city townhouse rather than amidst the rural farmland of Tijnje.

Next to nature

THIS CONVERTED CHURCH is positioned between the centre of Tijnje and a forest that grows right up to the back garden. It enjoys a very beautiful rural setting in a coastal region of the Netherlands called Frisia, or Friesland, which has its own language: Frisian. Maaike Goldbach grew up in the area and speaks a little Frisian, although Dutch is her first language. She shares her unconventional home with her husband Onno, a captain in the Dutch army, and their two-year-old daughter Amelie.

ABOVE The wide hallway has been beautified with art and flowers. Entrance halls are often overlooked, but with a little thought they can set the right tone for a home.

OPPOSITE Here you can really see the bones of the church and the sophisticated way in which it has been converted into a home. The neutral but elegant furnishings combine well with quirky details such as macramé plant holders and vintage lighting. A series of botanical prints adds a touch of nature.

The couple bought their home two years ago and were fortunate to find it in a very good condition. Built in 1910, the church was converted to a residence in 1996, when an architect was employed and the structure was altered to make the interior more liveable and modern. From the outside, it still resembles a village church, with a white plaster exterior and grey double doors. Inside, many of the original features have been retained, including the pulpit, which can be reached by a door in the master bedroom and looks down onto the living room. When two-year-old Amelie discovers it, no doubt it will become her favourite secret hideout.

The wooden floors are original to the building and add a rustic feel to the otherwise sleek interior. The large church windows, which Maaike describes as creating 'each season, a different painting', allow sunlight to flood the spacious ground floor, where white walls, curtains and furniture provide a clean canvas upon which Maaike can experiment with pattern and colour. She often begins with a piece of fabric or wallpaper, and uses this as a starting point to build a story around, adding complementary patterns but always keeping it from becoming too busy or hectic.

ABOVE In the kitchen, retro-style appliances contribute a sense of personality. The dining area wallpaper is repeated in the small room seen beyond the kitchen, giving a sense of continuity to the interior. The beautiful arched doorway echoes the shape of the large windows.

LEFT Throughout her home, Maaike has grouped treasured items together to create little vignettes. This one, on a windowsill in the living room, bears testament to Onno's love of nature – a branch, a feather, a couple of plants, all beautiful and organic in their own way. When clustered together, they are elevated to an artful installation.

Maaike has a stylist's eye for detail and her home is punctuated with little vignettes. Before having her daughter she enjoyed a successful career as a window dresser, travelling the country in a van and designing windows for different stores. On her travels she discovered many places to shop for her home, including vintage markets where she would hunt down unique pieces. Husband Onno is the more practical of the pair, favouring function over form. He loves nature and often brings home feathers, pebbles, flowers and other natural objects found when out running in the forest behind their house.

Maaike describes the wallpaper in the dining room as representing their two styles combined: Onno's love of the natural world and Maaike's passion for pattern and vintage.

What is so attractive about this home is the care and thought that has gone into it. Maaike and Onno have taken an unusual building and made it their own, while still giving a nod to its original use. The couple have lived in more conventional homes, but here in their little church in the countryside they have managed to find the perfect balance of nature, practicality, quirkiness and fun – in other words, something for the whole family.

OPPOSITE The grand proportions of this room demand a lamp on an equally grand scale. The neutral backdrop allows for easy updates with patterned textiles. White linen curtains pull back to reveal the forest behind the house.

BELOW In the master bedroom, Maaike has covered the headboard with vintage fabric. The modern wood lamp keeps it from feeling too retro. Behind the bed is the door leading to the old church pulpit.

OPPOSITE **A teepee made from world map fabric and three wooden posts is a cosy spot to read or daydream. Touches of black bring drama to the feminine scheme and cut the sweetness ever so slightly.**

ABOVE LEFT In Amelie's playroom, Maaike used a mix of untreated wood finishes, white surfaces and pops of bright emerald green. The birdhouse wallpaper and an ethnic rug add depth and interest.

ABOVE RIGHT The colour palette is strictly adhered to throughout the playroom, giving it a strong look. The mini wicker peacock chair is boho at its best and pairs perfectly with the brightly painted screen to create a cute little dressing area that would be envied by grown women everywhere!

RIGHT In the back garden is a small studio where the family can sit outside sheltered from the elements. An old bed has been converted into a sofa and layered with pillows and warm throws.

Retro riad

Designers Emma Wilson and Graham Carter bought this 200-year-old riad in 2002 and together converted it into the holiday home it is today. Set within the narrow streets of the medina in Essaouira, a breezy fishing port on the Moroccan coast, the house appears no different to its neighbours. But step inside and you are struck by a quirky mix of traditional stone arches, retro furniture and unexpected pops of colour. It comes as no surprise to hear that the owners were once proprietors of vintage furniture shops in London.

ABOVE In the kitchen, the couple experimented with *tadelakt*, a plaster finish typically used in Moroccan bathrooms and hammams. Renowned for its soft texture and water-resistance, it made the perfect surface for these moulded kitchen units. A large metal hamburger sign adds a hint of boho kitsch.

LEFT Rather than use hanging shelves and brackets, these examples were designed to be a part of the wall and a quirky feature in themselves.

DAR BEIDA, OR THE WHITE HOUSE, was the second house Emma Wilson bought in Essaouira. With Graham Carter, her partner at the time, she set about creating a cave-like, almost space-age interior, with curved walls and few hard edges. A complete restoration was needed, but the couple managed to retain the original features of the Moroccan riad, including the ceilings and stone arches. The couple now live in different houses (see pages 68–75) and Dar Beida is a holiday rental.

eal

THIS PAGE The home's original arches were revealed when the restoration took place. A small dining area is tucked between the arch and the kitchen, with a 1960s table and a sign purchased from a flea market in Marrakesh setting the tone.

The home is comprised of three floors and a roof terrace. As with all riads, it was built around a central courtyard that was once open to the elements. This is now enclosed but still allows sunlight to stream in. Stone archways lead from the small courtyard into rooms shaded from direct sunlight; and stone steps lead you up to the floors above until finally you are hit by a blast of white-hot sunlight on the rooftop.

At Dar Beida, Emma and Graham have managed to stay true to traditional Moroccan architecture and style while indulging their own retro tendencies. The end result doesn't feel forced and the two styles blend really well together. The best way to describe it is part-riad, part-1960s James Bond movie set and part-Hobbit home.

When you take away the splashes of colour that are introduced in the form of art, fabric and accessories, the backdrop is strictly neutral: whitewashed walls, stone arches and creamy beige-hued floors and surfaces crafted from *tadelakt* – a traditional Moroccan lime plaster finish often used in the hammams of Morocco and prized for its waterproof and decorative qualities. Here, it has been used for everything

OPPOSITE In one of the small living areas, a rustic wooden table is surrounded by bespoke white leather pouffes, and nestled close to the fire. The fire itself is a thing of beauty, seamlessly forming part of the wall.

ABOVE On the ground floor, in the centre of the home, a wicker chair hangs in front of an ancient arch, revealed when layer upon layer of paint and plaster was removed. The sign was found at a flea market in Marrakesh.

from kitchen counters to bathrooms and floors. It has an appearance similar to polished concrete, with a smooth, tactile finish and a soft feel underfoot. Emma and Graham chose a soft beige tone, but *tadelakt* can be tinted any number of colours.

Emma and Graham are avid collectors. They once owned furniture shops in London and over the years have amassed an impressive collection of vintage pieces. At Dar Beida there are two types of collection on display: one themed around the earthy and natural, with ceramics, wood, shells and other materials found in nature;

the other retro, with bright colours, painted metal, colourful plastic and flower power textiles. They have managed to keep the balance between the two just right, so the inteior is neither overwhelmingly kitschy, nor is it too rustic. Many of the pieces in their collections were found locally and on their world travels, including masks brought back from a trip to Zanzibar and retro pieces shipped all the way from London. There is also an array of stones, fossils and shells found by their young son on the beach and displayed with pride.

In the kitchen, the centrepiece is the custom-built kitchen unit with broad, deep shelves that are all slightly irregular in form. Something that could have just disappeared into the background

OPPOSITE ABOVE RIGHT
In one of the bedrooms, the 1970s are alive and well. Flower power fabric and a handmade wall hanging – simply string and shells knotted together – are all the adornment this white-washed bedroom needs.

OPPOSITE BELOW LEFT
A large potted plant soaks up the sun in the central space of the home, which was once a courtyard open to the sky above. The couple's love of vintage is evident, thanks to a pair of pouffes made from retro-style patterned fabric and a red geometric lamp. It isn't what you might expect in a Moroccan riad, but somehow it works.

RIGHT This heavily beaded armchair, typically West African, stands guard at the end of a bed and adds a burst of vibrancy to the tranquil room. When a room's base colours are neutral, you can easily update it by rotating a selection of colourful accessories.

ABOVE AND ABOVE RIGHT In this room, two cultures collide. The chair and table made from horns and animal hides (not everyone's cup of tea I know) are in stark contrast to the white plastic, mushroom-shaped lamp and the patterned curtains. Finding the right balance is the key. For this couple, they simply collect what they like and piece it together as they go.

OPPOSITE On the rooftop, a lean-to shelter provides respite from the hot sun. A tree trunk holds up the bamboo roof under which sits a stone table especially designed for the space.

has become a feature of the open-plan space and is visible from the dining area. The *tadelakt* finish has become more interesting with use, with some areas darkening and developing a rich, satiny finish. I've never subscribed to the idea of a kitchen having to be immaculate; obviously you want a clean and hygienic space, but a kitchen gets so much use that you are better off designing a room that improves with age rather than the other way around.

Most natural finishes such as wood and lime plaster acquire a beautiful patina with use, and look great when paired with practical, contemporary materials such as stainless steel.

At Dar Beida, traditional Moorish style has been cleverly married with an eclectic retro look for an interior that is organic, fun and completely unexpected. If you are planning a trip to Morocco, you would be hard pressed to find a more unusual place to stay.

Rustic simplicity

Designer Valentin Loellmann originally hails from Southern Germany, but has settled in the Dutch city of Maastricht. He divides his time between a small 18th-century house on the river Maas and his studio in an old hat factory. Valentin was raised in a family of artists, an upbringing that was instrumental in his development into the artist and designer he is today. His curiosity and desire for creative expression is evident everywhere in the home and studio he has built for himself.

ABOVE RIGHT In the studio, the table in the foreground is a work in progress. Behind is an impressive wall of drawers, each one with a different knob or handle and holding the tools of Valentin's trade.

LEFT Hazel branches, handpicked for their character and strength, await transformation into one of Valentin's benches or tables. To the left is one of his early designs, a cabinet made from old bangkirai wood and polyester.

ALTHOUGH WELL KNOWN AS A FURNITURE DESIGNER, first and foremost Valentin is an artist, seeking a means of expression in everything he does. Whether he is designing a desk or a house, the same rules apply: to connect, as he puts it, 'the past and the present, the old and the new, the natural and the artificial'.

Valentin has worked tirelessly for the past year to make this charming house overlooking the River Maas his own. He spent the first couple of months adding basics such as electricity and heating, and carrying out repairs to the roof. Once this boring but essential work was completed, he moved onto the more interesting task of making the space feel personal, blending the original features of the house with some new ideas. Being an ardent fan of plant life, he built a conservatory onto the back of the house; he now has a garden full of potted citrus trees that can survive the

THIS PAGE A simple way to create the illusion of a separate room within a bigger space is to build a wooden platform. Here, a mattress and a pile of pillows become a makeshift sofa. Examples of Valentin's and Jip's work are everywhere – the light, the tables and the illustrations.

THIS PAGE In the living room, which looks out onto the river, a pleasing mixture of old and new furniture is gathered in this corner, while one of Valentin's Drift lights waits to be hung. The décor is deliberately minimal, with only pops of blue as an accent.

OPPOSITE BELOW This small but very heavy table was made by Valentin. His work is organic and natural, but his method is entirely modern. He says that he creates furniture that looks like it might have grown that way in the wild.

cold Dutch winters. This has quickly become his favourite spot, warm and light even during the winter months and heavy with the scent of lemons.

Valentin shares the house with his girlfriend Jip Linkens, a fine artist who is currently working on an illustrated children's book and whose delicate watercolours are dotted all over the house. Their next big project is to remove the roof and add another bedroom overlooking the garden and the hills beyond. The home has a simple, rustic feel to it, but with a definite modern edge. Valentin's own furniture designs share the space with old chairs found at an antiques market in Belgium and classic designer pieces. The walls are white or very light and their surface is rough and uneven, a theme that's continued elsewhere.

In Valentin's studio, the sense of pleasingly organic imperfection continues. The floors are concrete, pitted and marked in places, and everywhere there is wood, with cut branches stacked in the corners and pieces of furniture in varying stages of completion dotted around the space. A wooden platform was built to create a raised lounge area, while the kitchen cabinets were roughly constructed from wood and stained black.

Decorating both his home and studio are pieces that Valentin has acquired through exchanges with other artists: photographs, paintings and antique furniture. He also has something from each member of his impressively creative family – photographs taken by his brother, ceramics crafted by his father, floor tiles made by his sister and a quilt stitched by his mother, to name just a few. Surrounding himself with the handmade seems to be a way of life for Valentin. If an object wasn't made by him, then you can be sure it was made by someone he knows.

ABOVE In the kitchen, Valentin built the wooden units himself – this one makes good use of a corner. Almost all his tableware is stored on the two deep, curved shelves. The kitchen's surfaces and cupboards were finished with the same black stain and wax as much of Valentin's furniture. Black-and-white photos form an impromptu gallery, loosely stuck up with tape so that they can be easily moved around whenever desired.

ABOVE Above the bathroom doorway a thick, rough plank is built into the wall, home to a couple of paintings by Jip. The rough, curved bathroom walls and the earthy green paint create a cave-like mood in the cool, dark space.

ABOVE RIGHT The hexagonal tiles in the bathroom were deliberately laid in an imperfect, wonky fashion, working with the lumps and bumps on the walls. Valentin uses an old ladder as a towel rail and – my favourite thing – a bevelled-edge mirror has been embedded into the wall.

RIGHT This warm and sunny area leads to the garden and is a pleasant spot for relaxing. The sleek black lamp stands out against the rustic vibe of the room.

OPPOSITE Valentin designed and built the conservatory, and now his citrus trees can thrive despite the long, cold Dutch winter. The long wooden bench has a beautiful patina from its exposure to the elements.

LEFT AND BELOW The architectural features of this 1960s home dominate the airy living room. Set on the first floor, this is Sara's favourite room, a space that makes her feel like she's sitting in the treetops. A large feature fireplace allows ample room for Sara to display favourite collections of pieces gathered on her many travels. The contemporary lines of the sofa are broken up by piles of kilim pillows, each one unique.

Scandi boho

In the Danish city of Odense, the birthplace of Hans Christian Andersen, lives Sara Schmidt and her family. Having travelled the world and enjoyed a varied career as a television host, art teacher, model and designer, Sara settled in this architect-designed home three years ago. She now runs a successful interiors company and online store, and her home serves as both a showroom and laboratory for her unique way of mixing ethnic pieces with Scandinavian architecture and style.

SARA SCHMIDT CUTS A STRIKING FIGURE. She is tall, stylish and elegant, but, with her hair cut in a cross between an undercut and a Mohawk and her vintage prescription glasses, she also has an edginess to her that I like to call punk chic. Her home shares the same cool combination of clean, elegant lines, layered with an unexpected edge. Sara's approach to decorating is to start with the classic bones of Scandinavian style and then to add a twist in the shape of what she describes as her 'unique ethnic findings'. These include restored kilim rugs

THIS PAGE The huge fireplace allows access from all angles and separates the main living room from a smaller seating area next to the bookshelves. Instead of lighting the fire, Sara sometimes fills the cavity with candles, which, when lit, create a warm glow without all the effort of building and stoking a fire.

RIGHT In Sara's compact kitchen, the floors and countertops are marble, a luxurious contrast to the oversized metro tiles on the walls and the specially designed cabinets. Sara's dedication to kilim rugs in every room can be seen here in earthy hues that tie in with the tone of the wood.

and pillows, sculptures from Africa and lassi cups from India, all of which she sells through her company Brandts Indoor.

The house was built in the 1960s by an architect who then lived in it and built smaller versions next door. A great deal of restoration was undertaken to bring the house back to its former glory, with special attention being given to using the same materials and design as the original. Warm wood and slate tiles are the primary flooring throughout and serve to ground the home. White is the paint colour of choice for most of the interior, with the exception of the master bedroom, which has walls of the softest celadon green.

The home is furnished with classic Scandinavian pieces, some vintage and some contemporary. Sara has then added finds from her buying trips, and it is this layering that gives the sleek rooms a boho edge. Kilim weavings play a large role in the interior, with a rug or pillow in every room. Sara sources kilims for her business and then has them restored. Those that are beyond repair are turned into one-of-a-kind pillows.

For Sara, it is important to get the balance right. Not enough pattern and textiles and the classic Scandi look can feel cold and stark;

RIGHT For her business Sara sources old kilim rugs that she then either restores or turns into pillows. Here, she has a selection that share a natural base colour with pops of pink and red. They add a sense of rich earthiness to a Bohemian Modern home.

LEFT In the dining room, a cosy seating area has been created under the stairs. A very low marble-topped coffee table is just the right height for a pair of large floor pillows. On the wall hangs a huge white feathered Juju hat, traditionally worn by prominent members of the Bamileke tribe in Cameroon.

OPPOSITE The dining room is where Sara's signature style is most evident: clean lines, classic Scandi design, one-of-a-kind treasures and black-and-white photography. Hans Wegner's classic Wishbone Chair looks completely modern in black and partners well with the softly patterned vintage rug. The large collage is one of Sara's own creations and is a work in progress.

too much and a room can look like Istanbul's Grand Bazaar. To create Sara's simple, eclectic look, the key is to have a few carefully chosen pieces. It's not about more is more but about finding the right pieces to keep a space elegant and interesting.

The living room is a perfect example. This large, airy space with its floor-to-ceiling wall of windows isn't overwhelmed with too many different patterns. Kilims introduce colour and pattern and warm the clean lines of the contemporary sofa. Throughout Sara's home, kilims are the thread that ties everything together.

Another common feature of the home is Sara's collection of black-and-white photography, some of it by Sara herself. She started her collection five years ago when she bought

a piece from a shop in Paris. Sara moves the pictures around constantly, a rotating gallery of sorts. Using black-and-white photography on the walls is a great way to maintain a cool modern edge, and it plays nicely against some of the more eclectic sculptures and artefacts on display.

Sara's home exudes calm and order throughout. Even though it is filled with intriguing collections and gorgeous textiles, these decorative elements are kept firmly in check and not allowed to become overpowering. It is Sara's innate ability to curate and edit that sets this house apart. For someone who travels the world constantly, the temptation might be to keep adding more and more. But this breed of sleek, clean-lined Scandi boho demands discipline and a focused eye, both of which Sara clearly has in abundance.

OPPOSITE ABOVE In Sara's studio, a corner is used to display moodboards. Stacks of pillows ready to ship to clients lean next to a simple white set of drawers that hold fabric. Notice the scale of the clock – oversized pieces add a sense of fun to any home.

OPPOSITE BELOW LEFT In her young daughter's playroom, Sara has mixed a white mini Panton chair with a collection of rugs and pillows. An African stool is just the right height for a tea party table, with a scarf acting as a makeshift canopy for the furry guests.

OPPOSITE BELOW RIGHT In the bathroom, the cabinets are by the same designer as in the kitchen. Marble floors add sophistication, while the tassels and trinkets bring a dash of charm and personality.

THIS PAGE In the master bedroom, the walls are painted a soothing green shade and the décor is simple and calming. The pillows provide some texture. Each one is unique and is sewn from a traditional Moroccan wedding blanket.

OPPOSITE The main living area stretches the depth of the home, from the narrow windows at the front to the wall of glass at the back. Light floods in from the glass roof above and the hanging bedrooms create different shadows depending on the time of day. Joris designed the stair risers so that they appear to be varying heights; an optical illusion, of course, but an unusual detail.

Just east of central Amsterdam is Ijburg, the district's youngest neighbourhood, made up of six artificial islands. Amid newly built homes of every shape and style sits this architectural gem designed and built by artists Nicky Zwaan and Joris Brouwers. A few years ago it was an empty lot, but now it is a warm, sustainable and stylish home.

A sculptural gem

JORIS AND NICKY DESIGNED AND BUILT their house almost entirely by themselves, but it is only upon reading Joris's blog documenting the building process that the full scope of the project becomes apparent. With the help of friends and family, the couple transformed a sandy, exposed plot without an architect or contractor. They bought the plot in 2006 on the newly developed 'floating islands'

of IJburg and, over the course of a couple of years, built their home from the ground up.

The land on which the house sits didn't even exist until the 1990s, when it was created by pouring vast quantities of sand into Lake Ijmeer. Ijburg was designed as a way to deal with Amsterdam's housing shortage, but without negatively impacting the lake's environment. Amsterdam is no stranger to

ABOVE In the kitchen, organic meets shiny, new and pastel. The wooden knife board was a gift from a friend, who made it by imbedding a magnet into a slice of wood. The pastel-coloured knives add a hint of femininity and softness to the cool-toned kitchen. Even the water purifier is beautifully designed – every detail counts.

building on and living on water, but unlike along the canals, where buildings date back centuries, the homes on IJburg are in their infancy.

Nicky and Joris were able to purchase the land that the house is built on when the city offered a small number of plots to individual buyers rather than developers. The couple were inspired by the newness of the site because 'everything we could imagine had the possibility to manifest itself'. Being designers and artists in their own right, Joris and Nicky were able to envisage and create a home that is visually striking as well as environmentally conscious and sustainable.

Sandwiched between the contemporary but uninspiring suburban homes that line the street, the faceted plaster façade of the house is broken only by a handful of narrow, rectangular windows, placed horizontally and in a seemingly random pattern.

ABOVE A net hammock and walkway connects the rooms suspended above the living room. The netting was sourced from a local theatre company and is industrial weight, so it can carry a reclining body.

OPPOSITE ABOVE LEFT A group of spheres nestles in the greenery. When it comes to collections, there are no rules – acquire what you like, and when you have three or more of anything, a collection is born.

OPPOSITE ABOVE RIGHT Cosy textiles add colour to the pale sofa and are within easy reach when a chill sets in. The pop of orange is one of a few accents that have been introduced throughout the home.

OPPOSITE BELOW In front of the window sits a Jetson chair by Swedish designer Bruno Mathsson. Designed in 1965, it has a timeless quality that doesn't jar with the modern interior and the jungle vibe.

OPPOSITE Joris used parallel strand lumber (PSL) to make this unique staircase and feature wall. The material is typically used for beams, lintels and other internal structures that aren't usually seen. Notice the stair treads made from different thicknesses of PSL to create a variation in the riser gap. Cut-outs in the wall provide a gallery for displaying Nicky's West African collections.

ABOVE LEFT On the ground floor, below the living room and with direct access to the back garden, is the office. A bare-bones room with concrete floors, a desk made of a long stretch of wood and lots of potted plants, it is part workspace, part greenhouse.

ABOVE RIGHT In the spare bedroom, a curtain is made from the same netting as that used in the hammock beyond. This joins the walkway that connects the two bedrooms.

RIGHT In a corner of the small spare bedroom is a writing desk, a classic Scandinavian chair and one of Nicky's glass pentagon sculptures.

In contrast to the minimal windows on the front façade, the back of the house is a wall of glass – multiple panes of differing shapes and sizes placed in a design that's reminiscent of a Piet Mondrian painting, although without the primary colours.

Set over three floors, the home is tall and narrow, with an open-plan living, dining and kitchen area on the first floor that enjoys impressive views of the lake. In the summer, Nicky and Joris swim in the lake, and in the winter they skate.

Within the straight lines of the home's footprint, the couple have designed an interior that is unique. They originally wanted a home with high ceilings, but then decided more rooms were a priority, so they designed 'hanging' bedrooms – white cubes that appear to be suspended but which are in fact cantilevered from the walls. These rooms open onto the glass wall at the rear of the house and are connected by a walkway made of thick black netting that hangs above the living room. Each bedroom has its own net hammock – a magical place to lie back and watch the ever-changing sky and lake.

The interior is sleek and modern, but also organic and filled with character. The floors are polished concrete, the stairs are roughly hewn wood, and the corners are filled with plants. Wooden stools and sculptures from Nicky's childhood in West Africa bring personality and soul, while plastic school chairs add a pop of orange, an accent colour that is carried throughout the home.

Nicky and Joris let their imaginations run wild when they designed this house. It's like something a child might draw, filled with fantastical ideas: hanging bedrooms, net walkways, hand-built stairs. As artists used to doing things their own way, the fact that Nicky and Joris didn't know the rules of designing a house allowed them to make up their own along the way.

OPPOSITE ABOVE LEFT In the master bathroom, a tiny window looks down onto the living room below. Laboratory taps/faucets were sourced for the basin.

OPPOSITE ABOVE RIGHT The bathroom was finished entirely in *tadelakt*, a Moroccan lime plaster with a waterproof finish and soft patina. Again, science lab taps/ faucets were used for the Japanese-style cedar bathtub.

OPPOSITE BELOW A narrow hallway connects the bedroom to the bathroom, with a walk-in wardrobe and storage space sandwiched in between.

THIS PAGE In their 'hanging' bedroom, Joris and Nicky designed a small cut-out in the ceiling to let in light from the glass roof above. The walls are made from adobe and straw, and regulate the home's humidity.

SOURCES

NORTH AMERICA

ALL ROADS
www.allroadsdesign.com
Textile art studio in Los Angeles specializing in handwoven wall hangings and other small goods.

ANTHROPOLOGIE
www.anthropologie.com
Stores all over the US and now the UK too. Furniture, textiles and homewares. Inspiring display and merchandizing throughout their stores.

BROOKLYN FLEA MARKET
www.brooklynflea.com
Two locations, one on Saturday one on Sunday. Great for furniture, antiques and interesting collectibles.

HERRIOTT GRACE
www.herriottgrace.com
Father-daughter duo selling one-of-a-kind handmade items for the kitchen – think hand-turned wooden spoons, cake stands and beeswax candles.

JUSTINA BLAKENEY
www.jungalow.com
Justina curates a bohemian collection from around the globe as well as designing her own collections of rugs, sofas, artwork and more.

MELROSE TRADING POST
Los Angeles
melrosetradingpost.org
Flea market held every Saturday at Taft Charter High and every Sunday at Fairfax High School (see the website for directions and current opening hours). Laid-back and small, this outdoor market is not necessarily for serious antiques hunting but is good for vintage art and smaller items.

POKETO
820 E 3rd Street
Los Angeles
CA 90013
213-537-0751
www.poketo.com
Nice selection of kitchenwares and small household items such as hanging planters.

ROSE BOWL
FLEA MARKET
1001 Rose Bowl Drive
Pasadena
CA 91103
www.rgcshows.com
Second Sunday of every month. I used to live just five minutes from the Rose Bowl flea and I've both bought and sold at this legendary market.

SMALL ADVENTURE
Los Angeles
www.smalladventureshop.com
Beautifully illustrated prints and paper goods inspired by nature by artist Keiko Brodeur.

TW WORKSHOP
Los Angeles
www.twworkshop.com
and
www.store-la.com
I fell in love with Tracy Wilkinson's handmade pottery, lighting and one-of-a-kind furniture when I visited her home for my first book, Modern Rustic.

WEST ELM
www.westelm.com
Online and all over the US and now the UK too. Good selection of clean-lined wooden tables, benches and storage baskets as well as ceramic vases and dinnerware.

WORLD MARKET
www.worldmarket.com
Dotted all over the US, these stores stock a budget-friendly mix of bohemian, industrial and rustic furniture, textiles and homewares.

UK AND EUROPE

EMILY HENSON
That's me. My styling and interiors portfolio is www.emilyhensonstudio.com and my lifestyle/interiors blog is www.lifeunstyledblog.com. I'm also on Instagram/Facebook @lifeunstyled.

ABIGAIL AHERN
12–14 Essex Road
London N1 8LN
+44 (0)20 7354 8181
www.abigailahern.com
Queen of all things dark and moody, Abigail stocks her shop with everything you need for a luxe bohemian modern home.

BELDI RUGS
www.beldirugs.com
I met Emma Wilson for this book and feature two of her Moroccan homes (see pages 68–75 and 124–131). She runs Beldi rugs, selling authentic Moroccan rugs of all kinds. Having wandered the souks with her, I can tell you she knows her stuff.

BLOOMINGVILLE
www.bloomingville.com
Danish brand stocking everything for the home, from tables and textiles to candles and lighting.

BRANDTS INDOOR
www.brandtsindoor.dk
Beautiful selection of pillows and blankets made from restored kilim rugs and Moroccan wedding blankets. Owned by Sara Schmidt, whose home is featured on pages 138–145.

CARAVANE
www.caravane.co.uk
The most beautiful collection of linen curtains, cushions and sofas, most notably their divan-style sofas layered with thin mattresses that evoke The Princess and the Pea.

EMERY ET CIE
78 Quai des Charbonnages
1080 Brussels
Belgium
+32 2 513 58 92
www.emeryetcie.com
Agnes Emery's Belgian design company sells the most exquisite selection of tiles, paint, fabric and furniture. We visited her home in Morocco, which was covered in the stuff (see pages 98–107). Visit the website for details of their showrooms in Paris and Antwerp and their stockist in the UK.

GRAHAM & GREEN
www.grahamandgreen.co.uk
My go-to for rugs, cushions and textiles for the luxe bohemian home.

H&M
www.hm.com
If you are on a tight budget, H&M has some really nice homewares, including pure linen duvet sets and loads of cushion covers for silly prices.

HOUSE OF HACKNEY
www.houseofhackney.com
These guys are more eccentric British glam than boho, but I love their 'more is more' approach to pattern and colour. Wallpaper, fabric, furniture, even towels – they've put their mark on everything for the home.

IKEA
www.ikea.com
For that modern pop of colour, you can't go wrong with a bit of Ikea. It's my go-to place for inexpensive sheepskin rugs and modern lighting. I'm an Ikea fan and not ashamed to admit it!

LA REDOUTE
www.laredoute.co.uk
A well-priced selection of rugs, lighting, bed linen and other home furnishings.

LABOUR AND WAIT
85 Redchurch Street
London E2 7DJ
+44 (0)20 7729 6253
www.labourandwait.co.uk
Well-designed, functional and timeless homewares, from rope doorstops to Welsh blankets.

MAISONS DU MONDE
www.maisonsdumonde.com
This French brand offers globally influenced products for every room. The light fittings are particularly strong.

MERCI
111 boulevard Beaumarchais
75003 Paris
+ 33 (0)1 42 77 00 33
www.merci-merci.com
Parisian home goods and fashion, mixing high-end with new emerging artists. Great styling and merchandizing.

SUNBURY
Antiques Market
Kempton Park Racecourse
Staines Road East
Sunbury on Thames
Middlesex TW16 5AQ
+44 (0)1932 230946
www.sunburyantiques.com
Two Tuesdays a month. Go very early to get the good stuff.

TOAST
www.toast.co.uk
Nice lighting and rugs.

UNTO THIS LAST
www.untothislast.co.uk
Very cool, modern furniture using only birch plywood.

VLISCO
www.vlisco.com
Vlisco is the original purveyor of Dutch wax fabrics, sold all over the world and fashioned into clothing in West and Central Africa. I like to buy their colourful prints and make pillows.

YOLLY FLORIST
59 Dartmouth Road
London SE23 3HS
www.yolly.co.uk
My go-to florist for shoots, events and weddings, Yolly is also a photographer with an incredible eye, and is super-stylish to boot. She will hook you up with the perfect boho-mod bouquet.

PICTURE CREDITS

All photography by Katya de Grunwald.

Endpapers The home of the interior architect Jeanpierre Detaeye in Ghent; **1** Sara Schmidt, owner and creative director of Brandts Indoor; **2** The home of Maaike Goldbach in the Netherlands; **3** Dorthe Kvist garden and interior designer, stylist, TV host, blogger and author; **4** Sara Schmidt, owner and creative director of Brandts Indoor; **5** The home of Emma Wilson in Sidi Kaouki, available to rent for photo shoots; **6 left** Dorthe Kvist garden and interior designer, stylist, TV host, blogger and author; **6 right** The home of visual artists Nicky Zwaan and Joris Brouwers designed and built by them in Amsterdam, the Netherlands; **7 left** Dar Beida available to rent throughout the year www.castlesinthesand.com; **7 right** and **8** The home of visual artists Nicky Zwaan and Joris Brouwers designed and built by them in Amsterdam, the Netherlands; **9** The home of the textile designer Kim Schipperheijn in the Netherlands; **10 above** The home and studio of Petra Janssen and Edwin Vollebergh of Studio Boot in the Netherlands www.studioboot.nl; **10 below left** The home of Emma Wilson in Sidi Kaouki, available to rent for photo shoots; **10 below right** The family home of the interiors stylist and author Emily Henson in London; **11** The home and studio of Petra Janssen and Edwin Vollebergh of Studio Boot in the Netherlands www.studioboot.nl; **12 above** The home of the textile designer Kim Schipperheijn in the Netherlands; **12 below** The home and studio of Petra Janssen and Edwin Vollebergh of Studio Boot in the Netherlands www.studioboot.nl; **13** The home of the designer Agnès Emery of Emery & Cie in the Medina in Marrakech; **14** Dorthe Kvist garden and interior designer, stylist, TV host, blogger and author; **15** The home of the designer Agnès Emery of Emery & Cie, in the Medina in Marrakech; **16 above left** Dorthe Kvist garden and interior designer, stylist, TV host, blogger and author; **16 above right** The home and studio of Petra Janssen and Edwin Vollebergh of Studio Boot in the Netherlands www.studioboot.nl; **16 below** The home of Maaike Goldbach in the Netherlands; **17** Sara Schmidt, owner and creative director of Brandts Indoor; **18** The home of the interior architect Jeanpierre Detaeye in Ghent; **19** The home of Maaike Goldbach in the Netherlands; **20** The home of Emma Wilson in Sidi Kaouki, available to rent for photo shoots; **21 left** Sara Schmidt, owner and creative director of Brandts Indoor; **21 right** The family home of the interiors stylist and author Emily Henson in London; **22 above left** The home and studio of Petra Janssen and Edwin Vollebergh of Studio Boot in the Netherlands www.studioboot.nl; **22 above right** The family home of the interiors stylist and author Emily Henson in London; **22 below left** The home of the interior architect Jeanpierre Detaeye in Ghent; **22 below right** The home of the textile designer Kim Schipperheijn in the Netherlands; **23** The home of the interior architect Jeanpierre Detaeye in Ghent; **24–25** The home of the textile designer Kim Schipperheijn in the Netherlands; **26 above and below left** Dorthe Kvist garden and interior designer, stylist, TV host, blogger and author; **26 below right** The home of the textile designer Kim Schipperheijn in the Netherlands; **27** The home and studio of Petra Janssen and Edwin Vollebergh of Studio Boot in the Netherlands www.studioboot.nl; **28 left** Dorthe Kvist garden and interior designer, stylist, TV host, blogger and author; **28 right** Dar Beida available to rent throughout the year www.castlesinthesand.com; **29** Dorthe Kvist garden and interior designer, stylist, TV host, blogger and author; **30 and 31 below** The home and studio of Petra Janssen and Edwin Vollebergh of Studio Boot in the Netherlands www.studioboot.nl; **31 above** The home of visual artists Nicky Zwaan and Joris Brouwers designed and built by them in Amsterdam, the Netherlands; **32 above left** The home of Emma Wilson in Sidi Kaouki, available to rent for photo shoots; **32 above right** The London home of the artist Bobby Petersen; **32 below left** The home and studio of Petra Janssen and Edwin Vollebergh of Studio Boot in the Netherlands www.studioboot.nl; **32 below right** The home of Emma Wilson in Sidi Kaouki, available to rent for photo shoots; **33** The home of the interior architect Jeanpierre Detaeye in Ghent; **34** The home and studio of Petra Janssen and Edwin Vollebergh of Studio Boot in the Netherlands www.studioboot.nl; **35** The home of the textile designer Kim Schipperheijn in the Netherlands; **36** Dar Beida available to rent throughout the year www.castlesinthesand.com; **37 left and right** The home and studio of Petra Janssen and Edwin Vollebergh of Studio Boot in the Netherlands www.studioboot.nl; **37 centre** The home of Emma Wilson in Sidi Kaouki, available to rent for photo shoots; **38 above left and below right** The home of the textile designer Kim Schipperheijn in the Netherlands; **38 above right and below left** Sara Schmidt, owner and creative director of Brandts Indoor; **39** Sara Schmidt, owner and creative director of Brandts Indoor; **40–41** The home of Maaike Goldbach in the Netherlands; **42** The family home of the interiors stylist and author Emily Henson in London; **43 above** The home of Emma Wilson in Sidi Kaouki, available to rent for photo shoots; **43 below** The home of the interior architect Jeanpierre Detaeye in Ghent; **44 above left and below left** The studio and home of the artist/designer Valentin Loellmann; **44 above right** The home of the interior architect Jeanpierre Detaeye in Ghent; **44 below right** The home of the designer Agnès Emery of Emery & Cie in the Medina in Marrakech; **45** The studio and home of the artist/designer Valentin Loellmann; **46 left** The home of the interior architect Jeanpierre Detaeye in Ghent; **46 right** The family home of the interiors stylist and author Emily Henson in London; **47 above left**, above right and below left The London home of the artist Bobby Petersen; **47 above centre** Dar Beida available to rent throughout the year www.castlesinthesand.com; **47 below centre** The studio and home of the artist/designer Valentin Loellmann; **47 below right** The home of the textile designer Kim Schipperheijn in the Netherlands; **48 left** The home and studio of Petra Janssen and Edwin Vollebergh of Studio Boot in the Netherlands www.studioboot.nl; **48 right** The London home of the artist Bobby Petersen; **49** The home of the interior architect Jeanpierre Detaeye in Ghent; **50–61** The home and studio of Petra Janssen and Edwin Vollebergh of Studio Boot in the Netherlands www.studioboot.nl; **62–67** The London home of the artist Bobby Petersen; **68–75** The home of Emma Wilson in Sidi Kaouki, available to rent for photo shoots; **76–83** The home of the interior architect Jeanpierre Detaeye in Ghent; **84–91** Dorthe Kvist garden and interior designer, stylist, TV host, blogger and author; **92–97** The home of the textile designer Kim Schipperheijn in the Netherlands; **98–107** The home of the designer Agnès Emery of Emery & Cie in the Medina in Marrakech; **108–115** The family home of the interiors stylist and author Emily Henson in London; **116–123** The home of Maaike Goldbach in the Netherlands; **124–131** Dar Beida available to rent throughout the year www.castlesinthesand.com; **132–137** The studio and home of the artist/designer Valentin Loellmann; **138–145** Sara Schmidt, owner and creative director of Brandts Indoor; **146–153** The home of visual artists Nicky Zwaan and Joris Brouwers designed and built by them in Amsterdam, the Netherlands; **160 above** Dar Beida available to rent throughout the year www.castlesinthesand.com; **160 below** The London home of the artist Bobby Petersen.

BUSINESS CREDITS

EMILY HENSON
www.emilyhensonstudio.com
www.lifeunstyledblog.com
Instagram/Facebook
  @lifeunstyled
Pages 10 below right, 21 right,
22 above right, 42, 46 right,
108–115.

BRANDTS INDOOR
Lindeallé 31
DK-5230 Odense M
Denmark
T: +45 6614 5343
E: info@brandtsindoor.dk
www.brandtsindoor.dk
Pages 1, 4, 17, 21 left,
38 above right, 38 below left,
39, 138–145.

JEANPIERRE DETAEYE
Interieur Projecten
T: +32 477 18 08 07
E: info@jeanpierredetaeye.be
www.jeanpierredetaeye.be
Endpapers, 18, 22 below left,
23, 33, 43 below, 44 above
right, 46 left, 49, 76–83.

EMERY & CIE
www.emeryetcie.com
Pages 13, 15, 44 below right,
98–107.

MAAIKE GOLDBACH
@fleursdamelie
E: fleursdamelie@hotmail.com
Pages 2, 16 below, 19,
40–41, 116–123.

DORTHE KVIST
Garden and interior designer,
stylist, TV host, blogger and
author of "Bliv ven med din
have" and "Byhaven, Kål
kartofler og kærlighed"
www.meltdesignstudio.com/blog
www.meltdesignstudio.com
Pages 3, 6 left, 14, 16 above
left, 26 above, 26 below left,
28 left, 29, 84–91.

VALENTIN LOELLMANN
www.loellmann.de
Pages 44 above left,
44 below left 45, 47 below
centre,132–137.

BOBBY PETERSEN
www.bobbypetersen.com
www.featuringfeaturing.co.uk
Pages 32 above right,
47 above left, 47 above right,
47 below left, 48 right,
62–67, 160 below.

KIM SCHIPPERHEIJN
E: kimschipperheijn@hotmail.com
Pages 9, 12 above, 22 below
right, 24–25, 26 below right, 35,
38 above left, 38 below right,
47 below right, 92–97.

STUDIO BOOT
workshop for image and type
Van Tuldenstraat 2
5211 TG 's-Hertogenbosch
The Netherlands
T: +31 (0) 7361 43593
  +31 (0) 6 5111 5618
E: info@studioboot.nl
www.studioboot.nl
Pages 10 above, 11, 12 below,
16 above, 22 above left, 27, 30,
31 below, 32 below left, 34, 37
left, 37 right, 48 left, 50–61.

EMMA WILSON AND
GRAHAM CARTER
Castles in the Sand
E: emma@castlesinthesand.com
www.castlesinthesand.com
Pages 5, 10 below left, 20,
32 above left, 32 below right,
37 centre, 43 above, 68–75.

EMMA WILSON
Castles in the Sand
www.castlesinthesand.com
www.beldirugs.com
Pages 7 left, 28 right, 36,
47 above centre, 124–131,
160 above.

NICKY ZWAAN AND
JORIS BROUWERS
www.nickyzwaan.com
www.houseofbouw.nl
Pages 6 right, 7 right,
8, 31 above, 146–153.

INDEX

ACKNOWLEDGMENTS

Thank you to the wonderful team at Ryland Peters & Small for once again taking a chance on one of my ideas. It has been an absolute pleasure to work with each and every one of you. Thank you to Katya de Grunwald for such lovely photography and for dealing with a gruelling schedule as we zigzagged across Europe on trains. Thank you to the amazing homeowners all over Europe who welcomed us into their stunning homes and let me pester them with questions. Thank you to friends and family, who have put up with my disappearing act while I made this book and who I hope will welcome me back to my social life with a very large martini. Holly, Eliott and Duncan – my siblings – and all my amazing in-laws and extended family, that means you. Thank you to my mum, Jocelyn Simpson, who always let me do whatever I wanted to my room, including my teen years when I drew a huge pair of eyes on the wall and plastered my wardrobe doors with hundreds of my own painted handprints (don't ask).

I've written this book in trains, planes, taxis, hotel rooms and once or twice in bed, when I thought I was dying from exhaustion. This has been a challenging year, but now that this book is complete I can look back and honestly say it has been an incredible experience. I have loved writing it just as much as I have loved travelling for it, but I couldn't have done either without the unwavering support of my husband Erick who became Mr Mum during my frequent absences, and a very good one at that. Finally thank you to my lovely children Ella and Johnny, who make it all worthwhile.